Math on the Menu

Teacher's Guide

Grades 3–5

Skills

Creating Combinations; Building Models; Describing; Comparing; Predicting; Generating, Organizing, and Analyzing Data; Making Charts; Measuring; Communicating; Drawing Conclusions; Reflecting; Recording; Reasoning and Proving; Computation Skills; Calculator Skills; Problem-Solving

Concepts

Combinations, Number Sense, Data Organization, Data Analysis, Spatial Sense, Area, Perimeter, Range, Mean, Mode, Computation, Estimation, Money Sense

Themes

Models and Simulations, Systems and Interactions

Mathematics Strands

Discrete Mathematics, Geometry, Measurement, Number, Pattern, Statistics

Nature of Science and Mathematics

Cooperative Efforts, Real-Life Applications, Interdisciplinary

by

Jaine Kopp

with

Denise Davila

LHS GEMS

Great Explorations in Math and Science
Lawrence Hall of Science
University of California at Berkeley

Cover Design
Lisa Klofkorn

Design and Illustrations
Lisa Klofkorn

Photographs
Richard Hoyt
Laurence Bradley

Lawrence Hall of Science, University of California,
Berkeley, CA 94720-5200

Director: Ian Carmichael

Initial support for the origination and publication of the GEMS series was provided by the A.W. Mellon Foundation and the Carnegie Corporation of New York. Under a grant from the National Science Foundation, GEMS Leader's Workshops have been held across the country. GEMS has also received support from: the McDonnell-Douglas Foundation and the McDonnell-Douglas Employee's Community Fund; Employees Community Fund of Boeing California and the Boeing Corporation; the Hewlett Packard Company; the people at Chevron USA; the William K. Holt Foundation; Join Hands, the Health and Safety Educational Alliance; the Microscopy Society of America (MSA); the Shell Oil Company Foundation; and the Crail-Johnson Foundation. GEMS also gratefully acknowledges the contribution of word processing equipment from Apple Computer, Inc. This support does not imply responsibility for statements or views expressed in publications of the GEMS program. For further information on GEMS leadership opportunities, or to receive a catalog and the *GEMS Network News*, please contact GEMS at the address and phone number below. We also welcome letters to the *GEMS Network News*.

Reprinted 2005.

Printed on recycled paper with soy-based inks.

ISBN-13: 978-0-924886-16-4
ISBN-10: 0-924886-16-1

COMMENTS WELCOME !

Great Explorations in Math and Science (GEMS) is an ongoing curriculum development program. GEMS guides are revised periodically, to incorporate teacher comments and new approaches. We welcome your criticisms, suggestions, helpful hints, and any anecdotes about your experience presenting GEMS activities. Your suggestions will be reviewed each time a GEMS guide is revised. Please send your comments to: GEMS Revisions, c/o Lawrence Hall of Science, University of California, Berkeley, CA 94720-5200. The phone number is (510) 642-7771 and the fax number is (510) 643-0309. You can also reach us by e-mail at gems@uclink4.berkeley.edu or visit our web site at www.lhs.berkeley.edu/GEMS.

Great Explorations in Math and Science (GEMS) Program

The Lawrence Hall of Science (LHS) is a public science center on the University of California at Berkeley campus. LHS offers a full program of activities for the public, including workshops and classes, exhibits, films, lectures, and special events. LHS is also a center for teacher education and curriculum research and development.

Over the years, LHS staff have developed a multitude of activities, assembly programs, classes, and interactive exhibits. These programs have proven to be successful at the Hall and should be useful to schools, other science centers, museums, and community groups. A number of these guided-discovery activities have been published under the Great Explorations in Math and Science (GEMS) title, after an extensive refinement and adaptation process that includes classroom testing of trial versions, modifications to ensure the use of easy-to-obtain materials, with carefully written and edited step-by-step instructions and background information to allow presentation by teachers without special background in mathematics or science.

Staff

Director: Jacqueline Barber
Associate Director: Kimi Hosoume
Associate Director/Principal Editor: Lincoln Bergman
Mathematics Curriculum Specialist: Jaine Kopp
GEMS Network Director: Carolyn Willard
GEMS Workshop Coordinator: Laura Tucker
Staff Development Specialists: Lynn Barakos, Katharine Barrett, Kevin Beals, Ellen Blinderman, Gigi Dornfest, John Erickson, Stan Fukunaga, Philip Gonsalves, Linda Lipner, Karen Ostlund, Debra Sutter
Financial Assistant: Vivian Tong
Distribution Coordinator: Karen Milligan

Workshop Administrator: Terry Cort
Distribution Representative: Felicia Roston
Shipping Assistant: Bryan Lee
Director of Marketing and Promotion: Matthew Osborn
Senior Editor: Carl Babcock
Editor: Florence Stone
Principal Publications Coordinator: Kay Fairwell
Art Director: Lisa Haderlie Baker
Senior Artists: Lisa Klofkorn, Carol Bevilacqua, Rose Craig
Staff Assistants: Trina Huynh, Jacqueline Moses, Chastity Pérez, Dareyn Stilwell, Stacey Touson

Contributing Authors

Jacqueline Barber	Linda De Lucchi	Catherine Halversen	Craig Strang
Katharine Barrett	Gigi Dornfest	Kimi Hosoume	Debra Sutter
Kevin Beals	Jean Echols	Susan Jagoda	Herbert Thier
Lincoln Bergman	John Erickson	Jaine Kopp	Jennifer Meux White
Susan Brady	Philip Gonsalves	Linda Lipner	Carolyn Willard
Beverly Braxton	Jan M. Goodman	Larry Malone	
Kevin Cuff	Alan Gould	Cary I. Sneider	

Reviewers

We would like to thank the following educators who reviewed, tested, or coordinated the reviewing of *Math on the Menu* and *Messages from Space*. Their critical comments and recommendations, based on classroom and schoolwide presentation of these activities nationwide, contributed significantly to this GEMS publication. Their participation in this review process does not necessarily imply endorsement of the GEMS program or responsibility for statements or views expressed. Their role is an invaluable one; feedback is carefully recorded and integrated as appropriate into the publications. **THANK YOU!**

ARIZONA

Kyrene de Las Manitas Elementary, Tempe
Jeanne Anciaux
Lori Conroy
*Alice Maro
Pam Parzych

ARKANSAS

Fox Meadow Elementary School, Jonesboro
Sharon Hill
Kay Martin
*Dr. Ruby Midkiff
Linda Simpson

CALIFORNIA

Washington School, Alameda
*Traci Alligrati

Marin Elementary, Albany
Kenneth Fujita
Marlene Keret
Diane Meltzer
*Sonia Zulpo

Antioch Middle School, Antioch
Leslie Adams
*Mark Balken
Joe Smyle
Lynette Wall

Creekside Middle School, Castro Valley
*Mary Cummins Bird
Victoria Mah
Scott Malfatti
Nancy Wilder

Windrush School, El Cerrito
*Joanne Chace
Nicola Furman
JoAnne Rubio
Martha Vlahos

Emery Middle School, Emeryville
Steve Hambright
Mark Sneed
*Letecia Trotter-Brock

Stanley Intermediate School, Lafayette
*Mike Meneghetti
Dixie Mohan
Jan Winter

Joaquin Miller Elementary, Oakland
Karen DeCotis
Jan Matsuoka
*Joyce Melton

Manzanita School, Oakland
Geraldine Ferry
Anna Gorman
*Ashley Keller
Hattie Saunders
Felicia Sexsmith

Markham School, Oakland
*Sharon Kerr
Lynn Martin
Margaret Wright

St. Elizabeth Elementary School, Oakland
*Christine Bertko
Jim Chaky

Ellerhorst Elementary School, Pinole
*Jody Anderson
Nancy Cabral
Trudy Jensen
Kathy Paulson
Nancy Richtik

Seaview Elementary, San Pablo
Charise Calone
Patti Fabian
Krista Hansler
Christi Silveira
*Barbara Taylor

COLORADO

Kunsmiller Middle School, Denver
*Juan Carlos Galván
Sandra V. Jaime
George Pullis
Patsy Trujillo

MICHIGAN

John Page Middle School, Madison Heights
Barb Buezynski
Kay Davis
Jackie Jones
*Mike Mansour
Ralph Shepard

MISSOURI

Mullanphy Botanical Garden Investigative Learning Center, St Louis
**Barbara Addelson
*Diane Dymond
Martha Eckhoff
Katherine Leslie
Effie Miller
Dawn Tofari

NEVADA

Our Lady of the Snows Parochial School, Reno
Ann Boeser
*Dave Brancamp
Teresa Kennedy
Vilia Natchez

NEW HAMPSHIRE

Milford Elementary School, Milford
Heidi Blake
Jennifer Maurais
*Carol McKinney
Kathy Parker

TENNESSEE

Cosby High School, Cosby
Steve Sharp

University of Tennessee-Appalachian Rural System Initiative, Knoxville
**Terry Lashley

Centerview Elementary School, Newport
Kathy Holt

Cocke County High School, Newport
*Missy Biddle
Sheila Huskey

Parrottsville Elementary School, Newport
Randy Winter

TEXAS

Birdville ISD, Haltom City
**Gail Knight

Haltom High School, Haltom City
Cindy Hostings

Haltom Middle School, Haltom City
Liane Lovett

North Ridge Middle School, North Richland Hills
Jennifer Ford

Murray Fly Elementary School, Odessa
Alice Derras
Sandra McAdams
*Kym Monacelli

Richland Middle School, Richland Hills
Shannon Reeves

WASHINGTON

Hearthwood Elementary, Vancouver
Kirsten Comish
*Susan Crawford
Sara Myers
Linda Roland

WEST VIRGINIA

Spencer Middle School, Spencer
*William E. Chapman Jr.
Shelba Fountaine
Barbara J. Keen
David Ruediger

*   On-Site Coordinator
** Regional Coordinator

Acknowledgments

Denise Davila created and conducted the first "Mmm Mmm Math" class at the Lawrence Hall of Science. As the name implies, the mathematics was presented to students in the context of food preparation, with a focus on measurement and data organization. This series of activities culminated with a snack after each one. This class extended over several weeks, and marked the start of this unit.

In local testing, we found that the food component was not very practical given classroom logistics and expense. However, the activity involving tostadas, with strong mathematics content and great student appeal, became the springboard for the *Math on the Menu* unit. The unit evolved into one with an emphasis on discrete mathematics, as well as expanding into number sense, data analysis, statistics, measurement, and geometry. To provide cohesion and a context for the activities, the story of the Rosada family emerged. The various options for the closing fiesta retain the possibility of a real food celebration that connects to Latin cultures.

We would like to thank Monica Torres at St. Elizabeth School in Oakland, California, and her lively class of second graders who participated in the development of the local trial version.

We would especially like to thank Karen Corzan, a veteran teacher, who was instrumental in the development of the national trial version. She and Jaine Kopp worked side by side with her class of fourth grade mathematicians at Park Day School in Oakland, California, to develop several major new activities. Karen's expertise, dedication, and high standards help make this "gem" shine. Her fourth graders—as well as Bob Rollin's fourth grade class—also grace the photographs in this guide.

Thanks goes to Tule Clow for researching maize, tortillas, and Latin foods, and to Lincoln Bergman who adapted her research for the "Behind the Scenes" section.

After teachers and students across the country "digested" the mathematics in this guide, their reviews added both substance and spice to the menu. Our thanks to all of you!

Thanks also to our GEMS crew who enhanced the guide in many ways—in particular, to Florence Stone, who did an expert job editing with a careful eye for the smallest details, and Lisa Klofkorn, the artist who created a lively, festive cover design complete with *papel picado* as well as all the artwork within to add a wonderful "flavor" to the guide.

Contents

Introduction

This unit tells the taste-full story of two family-owned Mexican restaurants to provide compelling and memorable mathematics learning experiences for students. Basic skills are practiced and key mathematics content is presented in an interesting real-world context. Activities are sequenced to deepen learning.

The Rosada family starts a restaurant that features a variety of tostadas. They ask the students in your class for help as they plan their menu, determine different combinations of ingredients, analyze costs and set prices, expand into combination plates, and figure out the best ways to arrange the kitchen, bathroom, and tables in their newest venture.

There is plenty of mathematics on the menu!
Taken as a whole, this unit serves up a well-balanced meal of pivotal mathematics skills and concepts. Students gain increasingly sophisticated and complex understandings of the concept of combinations which falls under the umbrella of discrete mathematics. Students also have many opportunities to work in the central mathematical (and scientific!) area of statistics as they collect, organize, and analyze data. The activities also greatly strengthen students' number sense with opportunities to use addition and multiplication skills in meaningful contexts—including with money, measurement, and geometry problems. The closing activities, in which students design the interior of a new restaurant, develop students' spatial sense and delve into the mathematical areas of geometry, measurement, and number. Throughout the unit, students are using a variety of problem-solving and mathematical-reasoning skills, and they communicate mathematically as they work collaboratively, have class discussions, and write in their journals. **For further definition and more information on the key math content areas in this unit, see the Overviews to each activity and the "Behind the Scenes" section for the entire unit.**

On page 6 is a Letter to Families which can be sent home with the students at the beginning of the unit. This letter helps to explain the activities to families which in turn helps strengthen the home/school connection.

For detailed information about how the mathematics learning in this unit supports new national standards in mathematics, see page 104.

Session-by-Session Overview

As *Math on the Menu* opens, the students are asked to help the Rosada family determine how many different tostadas that feature three toppings can be made from five possible choices of toppings. After making predictions, students work with paper models of tostadas and toppings to determine how many choices a customer at the restaurant would have. They debrief all the possible combinations and these are recorded on a class chart. Students are asked to explain and prove how they know with certainty that there are no other combinations.

In Activity 2, the Rosadas ask for your students' assistance to compute the cost of tostada toppings as well as analyze their pricing recommendations. In "Tostada Cost Analysis," students are given the costs for each tostada topping. They determine the cost for each of the 10 combinations, examining the range, determine the mean (average) cost, and look for a mode (most frequently occurring cost). In "Setting the Price," students learn that restaurants need to charge a multiple of the ingredient costs to cover other costs and to make a profit on the food they serve. In this case, students triple the cost. Finally, for their journal writing, students are asked to write a persuasive letter to the Rosadas advocating their recommended prices for a tostada. The activity focuses on number sense and place value, in the context of the high interest subject of money. Students practice addition and multiplication skills. They also generate, organize, and analyze data, and explore statistics-related concepts.

In Activity 3, students apply what they've learned about combinations to solve new problems. The Rosadas have decided to expand their menu to combination plates, selected from six items, and each item on the plate must be different. The Rosada family wants to know how many different combinations are possible. Two of their children have proposed solutions to the problem. If your students will start with Joaquin's Solution, they analyze possible combinations of two, given six items. If they will start with Juanita's Solution, they analyze possible combinations of three. In Session 2, "Out to Lunch," your students are given an allowance to spend at the restaurant. They calculate the cost of each combination plate to determine what they can select given their set budget.

In Activity 4, the Rosada family has just purchased a building for a new restaurant. Before the construction crew comes in to build the kitchen and bathroom, the family needs to decide on a floor plan, within some very specific limitations and conditions. In Session 1, the family asks for your students' assistance, and they become architects and designers. Partners present their floor plans to the class and explain their rationale. In Session 2, students solve another combinatorial problem as they help the Rosadas choose a color combination scheme for their new restaurant. In Session 3, with the new restaurant up and running, customers arrive in parties of eight. The tables need to be rearranged to accommodate them. Then, on a Saturday night, the family receives reservations and needs to determine a seating plan, knowing that even more customers will arrive.

In the closing activity—optional depending on your preferences, but highly recommended as a great finale—your class can put on its own fiesta, applying what they've learned and rewarding themselves for all their hard work! This can take many forms from a "make your own tostada" party to a potluck of favorite Mexican foods. This celebration can be just for your class or you may want to include students' families as well. We provide a number of suggestions to ease preparation, emphasize learning, and have a good time! Some Assessment Suggestions and Going Further activities (for the whole unit) are also provided at the end of the unit. If you try any of them with your class, please give us your comments!

As Math on the Menu *follows the business success of a Mexican-American family, it can serve as a vehicle to explore and celebrate Mexican culture in the classroom. It could be part of a thematic unit that teaches tolerance and cultural diversity.*

The activities in *Math on the Menu* build upon one another and provide many opportunities for students to apply what they have learned. The ingredients for an educationally successful unit are yours to enjoy. We hope you find these activities filled to overflowing with mathematics and learning—and that they are truly *muy sabrosa*!

Time Frame

The teacher preparation needed for each activity will take between five and ten minutes once the materials are created for each activity. Each activity uses overheads that need to be made only one time. For some activities, there are paper manipulatives that need to be made—again one time only. The other materials that you may choose to use include the classroom mathematics manipulatives such as plastic cubes, wooden blocks, etc. Many teachers have effectively used parents, aides, and volunteers to assist them with the initial preparation of materials.

Activity 1: Tasty Tostadas

Creating Tostadas	10–15 minutes
Discussing the Combinations	10–15 minutes
The Proof's in the Organizational System	15–20 minutes
Journal Writing	10–15 minutes

Activity 2: Money Matters!

Optional Warm-Up Activity	30–40 minutes
Session 1: Tostada Cost Analysis	
How Much Is That Tostada?	30–40 minutes
An "Average" Tostada Cost	10 minutes
Journal Writing	10–15 minutes
Session 2: Setting the Price	
Restaurant Pricing	10 minutes
Quote A Price	20–30 minutes
Journal Writing	10–15 minutes

Activity 3: Combination Plates

Session 1: Making Combo Plates!	
Joaquin's Solution	30–45 minutes
Journal Writing	10–15 minutes
OR	*OR*
Juanita's Solution	30–45 minutes
Journal Writing	10–15 minutes
Session 2: Out to Lunch	
Out to Lunch	25–45 minutes
Journal Writing	10–15 minutes

Activity 4: La Fiesta Restaurante

    Session 1: Designing Floor Plans

        Exploring the Floor Space   10 minutes

        Enter the Codes   5 minutes

        Design Time!   20–30 minutes

        Journal Writing   10–15 minutes

    Session 2: Colorful Combinations

        Five Paint Chips   10–15 minutes

        Adding One More Choice to the Mix!   15–20 minutes

        Journal Writing   10–15 minutes

    Session 3: Rave Restaurant Reviews

        Big Crowds for Dinner!   15–20 minutes

        Everybody Loves Saturday Night!   10–15 minutes

        Journal Writing   10–15 minutes

Activity 5: Fiesta Time! (Optional)   times will vary depending upon your choice of Fiesta

Sample Letter to Families

Dear Families,

We are beginning a new mathematics unit—*Math on the Menu*—that is designed to help your child develop an understanding of combinations, data organization, and statistics as well as to practice computational skills in context. Your child will be doing problems related to real-world situations that evolve from a story about a family.

Throughout the unit, the students are asked to help the Rosada family solve problems related to their family business. Initially, their business is a tostada restaurant. Students determine the number of tostada combinations that can be made with the restaurant's five ingredients, do a cost analysis of the tostadas, and finally propose one price for the Rosadas to charge for their tostadas. The restaurant's success paves the way to expand the menu, thereby creating additional combination problems.

When the Rosadas purchase a new site for their restaurant, students use measurement, geometry and spatial sense, and number sense to create floor plans for them. Students present their floor plans to the class, and then they write persuasive letters to the Rosadas explaining why their plan should be selected.

At the end of the unit, we will be having a fiesta to celebrate the students' work and learn more about the food and traditions of other cultures. Details will be sent out as we get closer to that date. In addition, your child will have homework during the unit. In most cases, the work can be done independently. At other times, we may ask your assistance, such as gathering data—the prices for food items—at your local grocery store.

I appreciate your support of your child during this mathematics unit. If you are able to assist with the unit in any way, please let me know. We value you as partners in your child's education.

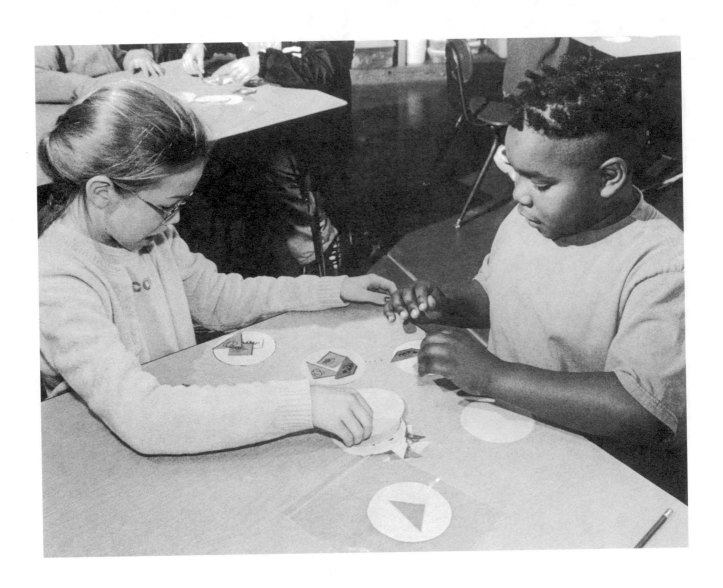

Activity 1: Tasty Tostadas

Overview

In the opening activity of the unit, students are introduced to the Rosada family, who have just started a business—the *La Tostada Sabrosa* Restaurant. (*Sabrosa* means "delicious" in Spanish.) The family is working on the menu. As the name suggests, the restaurant will feature tostadas, a popular dish with various ingredients, or toppings, placed upon a fried tortilla base. The restaurant offers five toppings—beans, cheese, salsa, lettuce, and olives. But each tostada can only have **three** out of the five toppings—and there can be no duplicate toppings! With these guidelines, students are asked to help the family determine the number of different tostadas that can be made, so they can be featured on the menu.

Students begin by making predictions about how many different tostada combinations can be made. Then partners work together with paper models of tortillas and toppings to determine how many possible tostadas the Rosadas can offer customers.

As students share their findings, the combinations are recorded on a class chart. Once the class agrees that all the possible combinations are recorded, they are asked to explain how they know with certainty there are no other combinations. Students collaborate with their partners to articulate proofs showing why there are only these 10 combinations—no more and no less. These proofs can be made by students designing charts, diagrams, or pictures, using mathematics manipulatives, or using any other tools or materials available in the classroom.

As students present their proofs, their classmates are given insights into multiple approaches to this problem. During the classroom discourse, it is likely that there will be many "teachable moments" to help students learn to use new tools to organize data. At the end of the discussion, student independently reflect on what they learned by writing in their journals.

This problem lays the foundation for additional combination investigations woven throughout this unit. The tostada problem has a finite, countable—or discrete—number of possible combinations that can be made. Combinations fall under the area of mathematics known as "combinatorics," which is a branch of discrete mathematics.

See the "Behind the Scenes" section on page 89 for a more detailed explanation of discrete mathematics and combinatorics.

What You Need

For the class:

- ❏ 2 overhead transparencies of the Tostada Combinations Chart (master on page 19)
- ❏ blank overhead transparencies
- ❏ overhead pens
- ❏ an overhead projector
- ❏ 6 pieces of 8 ½" x 11" paper in the following colors: tan, orange, red, green, and white
- ❏ 60 pieces of 8 ½" x 11" yellow paper
- ❏ 1 math journal per student or writing paper
- ❏ *(optional)* a variety of math manipulatives, such as unifix cubes, pattern blocks, tiles, etc.

For each pair of students:

- ❏ 1 set of paper tostada ingredients (see Getting Ready #3)
- ❏ 1 gallon-size ziplock plastic bag
- ❏ 2 copies of the Tostada Combinations Chart data sheet (master on page 19)

Getting Ready

You may also choose to make this chart on butcher paper and post it as a long-term reference for younger students.

1. Make two overhead transparencies of the Tostada Combinations Chart (master on page 19).

2. Duplicate the Tostada Combinations Chart data sheet (master on page 19) so each pair of students will have two charts.

You may want to make one set of enlarged tostada ingredients for the introduction of the tostada activity, particularly if your students have never seen or heard of tostadas before.

3. Create one set of paper tostada ingredients for each pair of students. Duplicate the sheet of each ingredient (masters on pages 20–25) on colored paper as follows: tortillas on yellow, beans on tan, cheese on orange, salsa on red, lettuce on green, and olives on white. Cut the ingredients from each sheet. For each set of ingredient manipulatives, place the following in a gallon-size plastic ziplock bag:

- 15 paper tortillas
- 10 paper lettuce
- 10 paper salsa
- 10 paper beans
- 10 paper cheese
- 10 paper olives

Writing provides an opportunity for students to consolidate and communicate their mathematical thinking using the language of mathematics and representations. It also provides a window on their understanding and as such is a valuable assessment tool.

4. **Writing Component:** Throughout the unit your students will be asked to write about the mathematics in each activity. For this writing component, decide if they will use special journals designed for this unit, an already existing journal, or sheets of paper.

5. Just before the activity, gather overhead transparencies and pens, student data sheets, and paper tostada ingredients, as well as any optional materials you decide to use, such as large charts, math manipulatives, and/or enlarged tostada ingredients.

GO !

Creating Tostadas

1. Take a brief class survey about tostadas by asking students if they have ever eaten one. Have a student who has describe it to the class, and let other students add on to that description. As they describe the tostadas, record the ingredients of a tostada on the overhead or chalkboard.

A tostada is a fried tortilla topped with a variety of ingredients—such as beans, cheese, and salsa (a spicy tomato sauce). Tostadas are served in many Mexican restaurants.

2. Tell students about the Rosada family—they are opening a restaurant called *La Tostada Sabrosa* ("Delicious Tostadas") that features tostadas. As they start up the business, they plan to offer a choice of **five** different toppings to go on the fried tortilla.

3. Using the list of ingredients the students generated, circle any of the following that are on it—beans, cheese, salsa, lettuce, and olives. If some of these ingredients are missing, add them to the list. Tell students that, at the onset, these are the five ingredients the restaurant will offer. Customers can select **three** toppings from the choice of five to go on the fried tortilla.

If you have decided to use enlarged tostada ingredients, identify and post them.

Depending upon your students' experience, the discussion on combinations may be very brief or extended to hear the strategies behind their predictions.

4. Tell students that the Rosadas have asked for their help in determining how many **different** tostada combinations can be made choosing three different toppings from the five choices. Emphasize that customers cannot have duplicate toppings, such as *cheese, cheese, salsa* or *beans, beans, beans*.

5. In pairs, have students discuss how many possible combinations they think can be made. Have them share their predictions and explain how they got them. You may want to record their predictions.

6. Tell students they will now work with their partners to solve the problem. Show them a bag of the paper tostada ingredients and explain these can be used as a tool to assist them. You may also want to make a tostada to demonstrate how the paper materials work.

7. Let them know that they can use these paper models of ingredients *or* any other classroom manipulative to help

them determine how many combinations there are. You may need to remind students that the tostada needs to have three **different** toppings—no double or triple amounts of the same topping are allowed.

8. Distribute the paper ingredients so students can begin work. Circulate and observe as they work on this problem. Ask questions and assist students as necessary.

Discussing the Combinations

1. While students are working, set up the overhead projector with the Tostada Combinations Chart. When students are finished, focus the class for a discussion. Ask them what strategies they used to solve the problem. Next, ask how many different combinations they were able to create. You are likely to hear several different answers.

2. Focus their attention on the Tostada Combinations Chart. Ask for one tostada combination. As a student gives three ingredients for a tostada, record it on the chart by putting an "X" in the empty grid boxes above the first tortilla. For example, if the three ingredients given are cheese, olives, and salsa, record as follows:

TOSTADA COMBINATIONS CHART

OLIVES	X											
LETTUCE												
SALSA	X											
CHEESE	X											
BEANS												

3. Have partners check to see if they have that combination. If not, they can build a tostada with those items.

4. Ask for a different combination. Record it on the chart. Again, have students check that they also have that combination. Continue this process, being sure to call on different pairs of students for combinations. Have the class check to be sure there are no duplicates as new combinations are given.

5. When they think there are no other possible combinations, count how many combinations there are. There are 10 possible combinations—however, **refrain from telling students this information!** Continue the problem solving **regardless** of whether or not students got all 10 combinations.

   a. If they all got the 10 combinations, ask students to prove to you and each other that there are no additional combinations. They need to make convincing arguments and explain how they are certain there are 10 and only 10.

   b. If they do not come up with the 10, ask students to explain how they can be certain that they have determined all the combinations. Again, they need to prove to you and each other with a convincing argument that there are no other possibilities.

6. As students set out to work on their explanations, make available the copies of the Tostada Combinations Chart data sheets to assist them, as well as any other classroom materials they'd like to use.

7. As students work with their partners, listen to the different strategies that they use to create their proofs. Ask questions that help students clarify their thinking.

When students work out a way to prove how many combinations there are, they are learning to reason and present valid arguments. This is an important part of understanding the mathematics behind the problem.

The Proof's in the Organizational System

1. When students have finished, have them present their solutions. Ask them to come to the front of the class and articulate their strategies. Make the overhead projector and blank transparencies available as a tool. Provide time for other students to ask questions. Find out if any other students solved it in a similar way.

2. Next, have students with a different strategy present their solutions. Point out that these are multiple solutions to the same problem. After all the solutions have been discussed, ask if there is one solution that seems best and why.

3. As a wrap up or at an opportune time when they discuss their proofs, look at the class chart again. Ask if it is organized in a way that helps them interpret the information on it. Why or why not?

4. Take this opportunity to show students an organizational strategy that can be applied to this problem. Use the second Tostada Combinations Chart overhead as follows:

a. Record a first tostada of *beans, cheese, salsa*.

b. Next, keeping the beans and cheese constant, record the next two possible combinations—*beans, cheese, lettuce*—and *beans, cheese, olives*—as follows:

TOSTADA COMBINATIONS CHART

OLIVES			X									
LETTUCE		X										
SALSA	X											
CHEESE	X	X	X									
BEANS	X	X	X									

c. Students should begin to see the organizational system. Ask what tostada to record next and why. Record it—*beans, salsa, lettuce*. Follow this with *beans, salsa, olives*.

d. Ask if there are any additional tostadas that can be made with beans. [The remaining one is *beans, lettuce, olives*.] How many possible tostadas were made with beans as one ingredient? [6]

e. Ask what should follow in this recording system. Listen to their ideas. Record a *cheese, salsa, lettuce* tostada. Ask what tostada would be next. It's *cheese, salsa, olives*. Are there other possible tostadas that have cheese as a topping? [*cheese, lettuce, olives*]

f. Look at the chart. Are there any other possible tostadas that can be made with the five toppings? Why or why not? [There is one last one—*salsa, lettuce, olives*.] This is how the chart will look when it is organized in this way:

See the "Behind the Scenes" section on page 89 for additional ways to organize the tostada combinations.

TOSTADA COMBINATIONS CHART

OLIVES			X		X	X		X	X	X		
LETTUCE		X		X		X	X		X	X		
SALSA	X			X	X		X	X		X		
CHEESE	X	X	X				X	X	X			
BEANS	X	X	X	X	X	X						
	◯	◯	◯	◯	◯	◯	◯	◯	◯	◯	◯	◯

5. Have students discuss the chart with their partners. Pose questions such as:

- What observations can you make about the chart?

- How many times is each ingredient used on the chart?

- Does it prove with certainty that there are no other combinations? Why or why not?

- Are there any other ways to organize the combinations to prove that there are only 10?

- Was it easier to use the paper ingredients or the chart to determine the combinations? Explain why that tool made it easier.

Journal Writing

Pose the following question or one of your own for students to respond to as they reflect on this activity. Their responses will inform your teaching in subsequent activities in this unit.

What strategies helped you to find all the tostada combinations and prove that you had found them all? Use illustrations, diagrams, or pictures to support your explanations.

> Elaya
>
> The strategies I used were Make a chart or graph and Use your mind and logic. The chart that I used helped me because a good piece of information was that you used each food item six times. I counted six in each row and that told me that there were ten combinations.

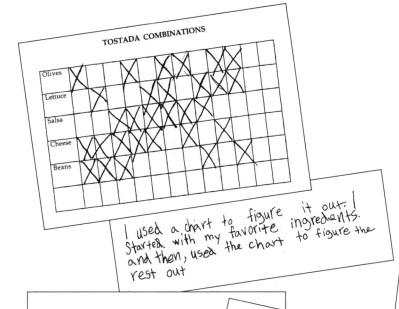

TOSTADA COMBINATIONS

Olives								
Lettuce								
Salsa								
Cheese								
Beans								

I used a chart to figure it out. I started with my favorite ingredients. and then, used the chart to figure the rest out

---

Anne

I liked the tree diagram because it was cool how it used the letters. It also helped understand the problem.

O L S C B

O-L = $\begin{cases} C \\ B \end{cases}$ 3
O-S < $\begin{matrix} B \\ C \end{matrix}$ 2
O-C-B 1
L-S < $\begin{matrix} B \\ C \end{matrix}$ 2
L-C-B 1
S-C-B 1
‾‾‾‾
10

· 1. olives
· · 2. lettuce   Suraya
· 3. salsa
· · 4. cheese
· 5. beans

1. 1,2,3 }
2. 1,2,4 } 1,2's   1. 6
3. 1,2,5   2. 6
4. 1,3,4 }   3. 6
5. 1,3,5 } 1,3's   4. 6
6. 1,4,5 — 1,4's   5. 6
7. 2,3,4 }
8. 2,3,5 } 2,3's
9. 2,4,5 — 2,4's
10. 3,4,5

Suraya   2/14/00

First, I numbered each ingredient. Olive, one; lettuce, two; salsa, three; cheese, four; and beans, five.
I started with one, and went in consecutive numbers, so the first one would be one, two, and three. Then, I kept the one and two and went to four, and then to five. So now we're done with the one, twos. I continued to use this pattern until I got six of each kind.

Sophia

(1) O-C-L
(2) B-O-L
(3) B-C-O
(4) S-C-L
(5) S-O-B
(6) S-O-L
(7) C-B-L
(8) B-C-S
(9) L-S-B
(10) C-S-O

Key
S = Salsa
C = cheese
L = Lettuce
O = Olives
B = Beans

Riley

I made a chart where there were five ingredients but you could only have three. I did 1,2,3 1,2,4 1,2,5 1,3,4 1,3,5 1,4,5 that's all the ones so I went on to. twos. 2,3,4 2,3,5 2,4,5 & 3,4,5.

Math

I used a key that means that I put down S=salsa/C=cheese/ L=Lettuce/O=Olives/B=Beans and came up with 10 posible ways that you can make a Tostada Combination. I did the O and got every combination and then the L and got all the combinations.

Going Further

1. The GEMS guide, *Group Solutions, Too!,* has a family of logic problems called Create A Creature that involve combinations. After doing this activity, you may want to do some of the problems from that guide.

2. Create A Combo Book. Have students create their own combination books modeled after combinatorial flip books such as *Por-gua-can* by Sara Ball or *Very Mixed-Up Dinosaurs* by Ian Jackson. To assist them, make a master sheet that is divided into three sections by two dotted lines. Mark the places where the bodies will connect so that the animals will line up when the book is put together.

Decide how many pages the books will be. Duplicate that number of pages for each student. Students will draw one animal per sheet. When they have created all their animals, have them cut along the dotted lines (which end before the left edge of the paper so that the pages can be stapled together without losing any of the picture). Place a cover sheet on top of the animal sheets and staple along the left side.

Have students determine how many different animals they can make with their books. Provide time for students to share their books with each other and their families.

3. Tortillas. Either have students research the history of tortillas or share information about tortillas with them (see "Behind the Scenes," page 89). Brainstorm other foods that use the tortilla as an integral ingredient—for example, chips and salsa, nachos, quesadillas, tacos, and enchiladas. Take a survey of students' favorite ways to eat tortillas, and have students create graphs with that data.

4. This activity combines aspects of what students learned in Activity 1. It can also serve as an assessment (see "Assessment Suggestions," page 112).

Ice Cream Parlor. The Cool Breeze ice cream parlor is promoting six flavors of ice cream—vanilla, chocolate, mint, coffee, butter pecan, and strawberry.

   a. Three-Scoop Cone Special—The ice cream parlor is selling three-scoop cones for the same price as a two-scoop cone—as long as a customer tries three different flavors. Ask your students: "If you ordered a three-scoop cone, how many different ice cream combina-

tions are there to choose from?" Tell them to explain their answer and be sure to use charts, pictures, or diagrams to illustrate their solution. They should explain why they are certain there are no other choices. Which three-scoop combination would they choose?

b. Sundae Special—Tell students that in addition to the three-scoop cones, there is also a special on sundaes. Sundaes are made with two scoops of different flavors of ice cream and a choice of topping—either chocolate fudge or caramel. Ask, "How many different two-scoop sundaes are there to choose from?" Students should explain their answer. Which "Sundae Special" would they choose?

Lacee

What did you learn about combinations?

Today in math we studied combinations. We had 5 different toppings for our tortilla. They were lettuce, salsa, beans, cheese, and olives. We discovered that we could use each one only 6 times to get 10 different combinations. The chart below shows the 5 toppings and the different combinations

	1	2	3	4	5	6	7	8	9	10
beans	X			X	X			X	X	X
lettuce	X	X				X	X	X		
cheese	X		X					X	X	X
olives		X	X	X			X			X
salsa			X	X	X	X	X		X	

what did you learn about combos?

Well I learned there are many different stradiges to make different combos I also learned that charts are a good way to do it.

Samia

What I learned about Organizing Data:
That you have to at least do a chart (put together pretty nicely) and then do a quite good check to be sure your answer is correct.

Jesse

You have to be clear Look for patterns.

Hannah

TOSTADA COMBINATIONS CHART

OLIVES												
LETTUCE												
SALSA												
CHEESE												
BEANS												
	🥟	🥟	🥟	🥟	🥟	🥟	🥟	🥟	🥟	🥟	🥟	🥟

OLIVES												
LETTUCE												
SALSA												
CHEESE												
BEANS												
	🥟	🥟	🥟	🥟	🥟	🥟	🥟	🥟	🥟	🥟	🥟	🥟

BEANS

CHEESE

SALSA

LETTUCE

OLiVES

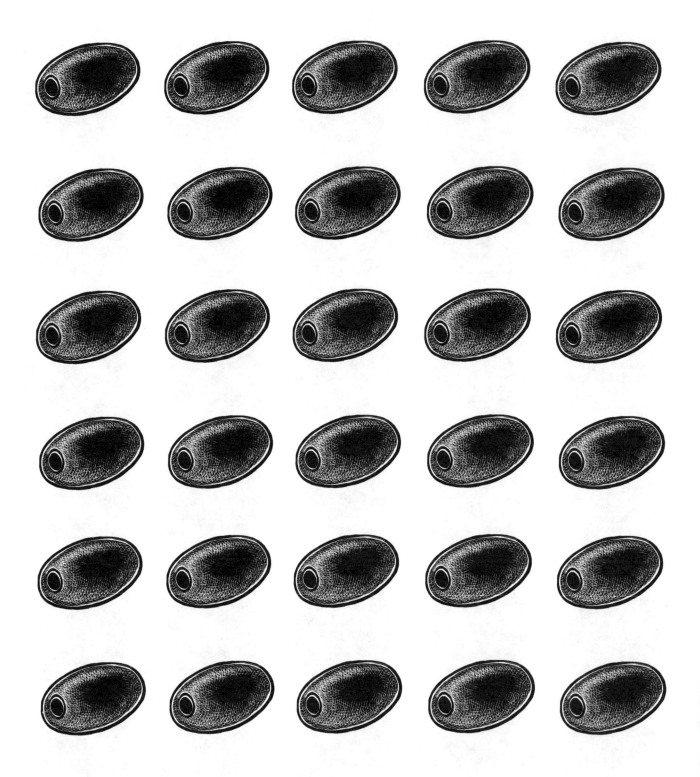

TORTILLAS

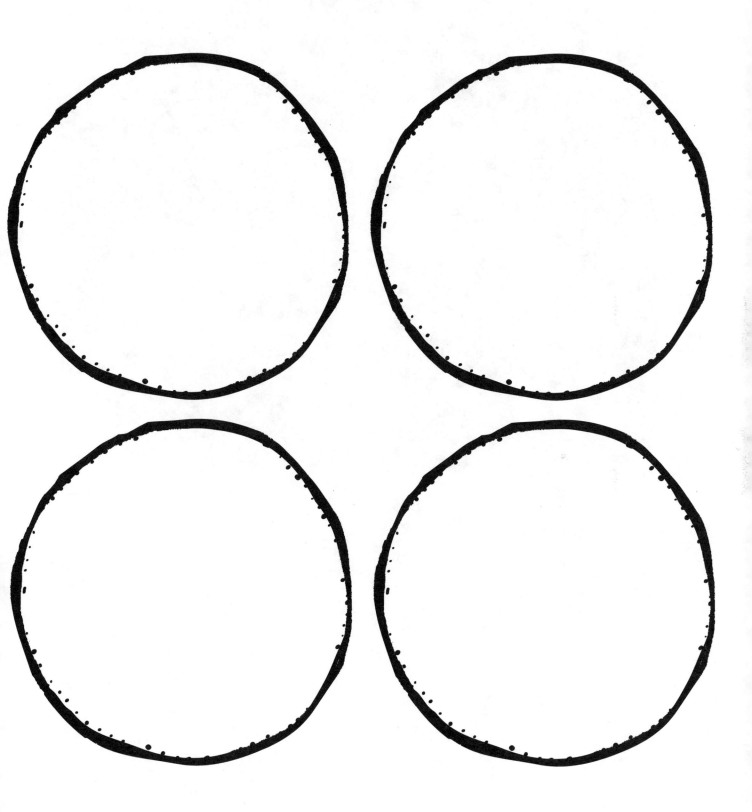

Activity 2: Money Matters!

Overview

The Rosada's restaurant, *La Tostada Sabrosa*, has enjoyed tremendous success, and the family is interested in analyzing how the restaurant is doing financially. In this activity, the Rosadas ask for your students' assistance in calculating the cost of tostada toppings as well as for advice on a price to charge for *any* tostada, regardless of the toppings chosen.

To prepare students for the mathematical averaging in this session, there is an optional "hands-on" Warm-Up activity in which students determine an average hand size for the class. They first estimate the length of their hand-spans in centimeters and then measure that length with centimeter cubes. Using cubes, the average hand-span can be determined in a concrete, non-abstract way. The students also discuss real-world connections to this measurement.

With third grade students—or other students who have not had a lot of experience calculating averages— you may want to do several concrete activities before Session 1.

In the first session of this activity, "Tostada Cost Analysis," students determine the cost for each of the 10 tostada combinations, including the additional cost of the tostada base. These costs are the data that students examine to focus on the range and distribution including the mode and median. Finally, they find the mean (average) cost, and compare it to the cost of all the tostada combinations.

In the next session, "Setting the Price," students learn restaurants need to charge a multiple of their ingredient costs to cover costs (rent, utilities, salaries, etc.) and make a profit. In this case, students triple the costs for each tostada combination to help them determine and advise the Rosadas on a single price to charge for their tostadas— regardless of the combination a customer chooses.

In this activity, students generate, organize, and analyze data, and then they apply the information from the data analysis to solve a problem in a real-world context. In the process they have opportunities to develop an understanding of averages, practice computational skills as well as use a calculator when appropriate. Number sense and place value are embedded as they work. Discourse is fostered as students are asked to explain their thinking and ask questions of one another to get at mathematical understanding.

See the "Behind the Scenes" section on page 89 for more information on data analysis and statistics.

What You Need

For the class:
- ❏ 1 overhead transparency of the Tostada Combinations Chart (from Activity 1)
- ❏ 1 overhead transparency of the Tostada Ingredient Costs (master on page 38)
- ❏ 1 overhead transparency of the Tostada Cost Chart (master on page 39)
- ❏ blank overhead transparencies
- ❏ overhead pens
- ❏ an overhead projector
- ❏ class journals or writing paper
- ❏ *(optional)* centimeter, unifix, or multilink cubes
- ❏ *(optional)* containers for cubes

For each pair of students:
- ❏ 1 Tostada Cost Chart data sheet (master on page 39)
- ❏ *(optional)* 1 calculator

Getting Ready

1. Decide if you will do the Warm-Up activity with your students. We suggest you use snap-together centimeter cubes for greater accuracy as well as to work with a standard unit of measure. You will need about 20 centimeter cubes per student. Alternately, you can use unifix or multilink cubes and you will need fewer. Fill containers with cubes that can be easily distributed so that small groups of students can measure their hands.

2. Make an overhead transparency of the Tostada Ingredient Costs (master on page 38). Depending upon your students' skills and abilities, decide the costs and record them on the overhead transparency. Here is one possible set of prices:

Tostada Ingredient Costs

Olives	35¢
Lettuce	15¢
Salsa	25¢
Cheese	65¢
Beans	25¢
Fried Tortilla	10¢

TOSTADA INGREDIENT COSTS

OLIVES	_____ ¢
LETTUCE	_____ ¢
SALSA	_____ ¢
CHEESE	_____ ¢
BEANS	_____ ¢
TORTILLA	_____ ¢

3. Once you have decided on prices for ingredients, fill them in on the Tostada Cost Chart (master on page 39). Make an overhead transparency and one copy for each pair of students.

4. Decide if you want to have calculators available, and if so, have at least one for each pair of students.

5. Just before the activity, gather the Tostada Ingredient Costs and Tostada Cost Chart overheads, as well as the Tostada Combinations Chart from Activity 1. Also have the overhead pens and student data sheets at hand.

Optional Warm-Up Activity: Hand-Spans

1. Ask students what they know about *averages.* Discuss how averages are used.

2. Have pairs of students compare their hand sizes by measuring hand-to-hand. Have them make observations about the relative size of their hands.

3. Define a hand-span as the distance from the tip of the thumb to the tip of the pinkie when the hand is spread to its widest point. Ask students to estimate that length on their hands in centimeters. Provide a point of reference for a centimeter.

4. Listen to their estimates and record them on the overhead or chalkboard. Have students determine the lowest and highest estimates and discuss the range.

5. Have students estimate the span of your hand. Demonstrate how to measure it in centimeter cubes.

6. Distribute containers of cubes and have students measure their hand spans. Next, have them compare the actual span to the estimated span. How close did they come?

7. Have students compare their hand spans with other students near them. Do any students share the same span?

8. Determine the shortest hand span in the class. Have that student bring his "train" of cubes to the front of the room where all students can see it.

9. Determine the longest span and again have that student bring the cube train to the front of the room. The longest and shortest trains represent the range endpoints.

TOSTADA COST CHART

OLIVES	35¢								
LETTUCE	15¢								
SALSA	25¢								
CHEESE	65¢								
BEANS	25¢								
TORTILLA	10¢								
TOTAL COST									

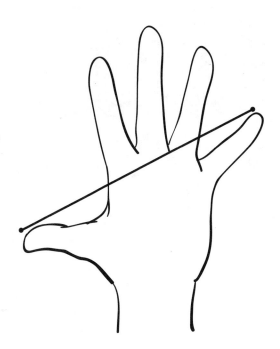

The chalk ledge works well to line up the cube trains. Place the shortest train at one end and the longest at the opposite end. Then the other lengths can be added inbetween.

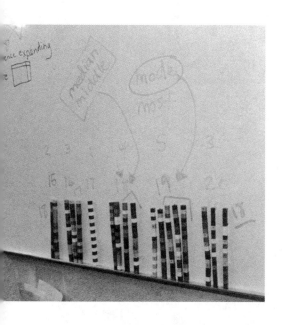

10. Continue by placing the additional trains between the range from shortest to longest.

11. Have students make observations about the data. You may want to provide statistical vocabulary, such as the *median* (number in the center of the data) and determine it for the hand-span data. Similarly, define the *mode* (the most frequently occurring number or numbers) and identify any mode(s) in the data.

12. Ask students what they think the average span of a hand is. Provide time for students to discuss this with a partner and share their thinking.

13. Ask how the cubes could be used to determine the average. Demonstrate how to do so: even out the cube trains by taking some cubes off the longer trains and adding them to the shorter trains. Continue until most trains are the same length.

14. Determine the average span. Ask for another way to determine the average without cubes. [Add all the hand-span measurements and divide by the number of people who measured their span.] You may want to use calculators to model how to determine the average. This will also provide a "check" for the concrete method of averaging.

15. Ask students who they think would be interested in this measurement and why. [Manufacturers of sports equipment, clothing, gloves, and medical products.]

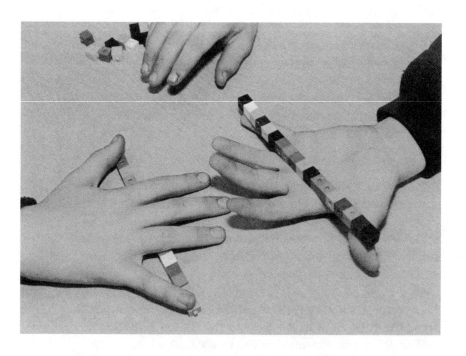

Session 1: Tostada Cost Analysis

How Much Is That Tostada?

1. Continue the story about the Rosada family and their restaurant.

   a. Tell students that when they first began, the Rosadas decided to sell each of their tostadas for the same price, regardless of the combination of toppings a customer selected.

   b. Now that the business has been going along successfully, they want to know how much each of the different tostadas actually costs to prepare, so they can analyze their profit margin and adjust the cost as necessary.

   c. Again, they are asking your students to help them with this problem.

   d. Based on the costs of the ingredients, they want to know how much each tostada costs to prepare. Then, based on what students advise them to do, the Rosadas may need to change their prices.

2. Put the Tostada Ingredient Costs transparency on the overhead and point out the prices of the ingredients, including the cost of the tostada shell. Ask what is the most/least expensive ingredient. Tell students they are going to use these prices to calculate the cost of the tostada combinations.

3. Put the Tostada Cost Chart transparency on the overhead. Model how to calculate the cost of the combinations. Fill in the cost of each ingredient for the first combination. Have students mentally calculate the total cost. Fill in the cost on the chart.

TOSTADA INGREDIENT COSTS

OLIVES	35¢
LETTUCE	15¢
SALSA	25¢
CHEESE	65¢
BEANS	25¢
TORTILLA	10¢

TOSTADA COST CHART

OLIVES	35¢						
LETTUCE	15¢						
SALSA	25¢	25					
CHEESE	65¢	65					
BEANS	25¢	25					
TORTILLA	10¢	10					
TOTAL COST		125					

TOSTADA COST CHART

	Price	1	2	3	4	5	6	7	8	9	10
OLIVES	35¢										
LETTUCE	15¢										
SALSA	25¢	25									
CHEESE	65¢	65									
BEANS	25¢	25									
TORTILLA	10¢	10									
TOTAL COST		125	115	135	.75	.95	.85	115	135	125	85

If the data contains an even number of statistics, there will be two medians.

4. Tell students they will work with a partner to determine the cost for all the tostadas. Put the Tostada Combinations Chart from Activity 1 on the overhead for students to refer to as they determine the cost for each of the 10 combinations.

5. Distribute the Tostada Cost Chart data sheet to each pair of students. Circulate as the students are working to observe the techniques and tools that they use.

6. When they have finished, record the total cost of each combination on the Tostada Cost Chart overhead transparency.

7. Have students make observations about the costs. Ask for the least expensive tostada combination and how much it costs. In contrast, what are the ingredients in the most expensive combination? How much does it cost? They may point out a cost that occurs more than once.

8. As they are making observations, take the opportunity to look at the data and ask students for ways to organize it. Through a class discussion, organize the data from lowest to highest. Here is one method of organizing the data calculated using the prices suggested in the Getting Ready section:

```
        85          115  125  135

  75  85  95  115  125  135
```

9. Encourage students to note the range, the number(s) in the center of the data (median) and those that occur more than one time (modes).

An "Average" Tostada Cost

1. Have partners discuss what an average is and how averages are used. Ask students how an average would help to advise the Rosadas on a single price for any combination.

2. Have students estimate an average cost for the tostada combinations. Listen to their estimations as well as to how they determined them.

3. Ask students to explain how to calculate the average. Have them work with their partners to determine the *average* or *mean* cost. Circulate as students work.

For young students, you may want to have plastic coins available to determine the average concretely.

4. Focus the class and ask students for the average cost of tostada combinations. Be sure there is consensus on the average cost!

5. Refer back to the cost of each of the 10 different combinations. Have students note where the average fits into the organized data, particularly how the average relates to the center of the data, and any modes.

6. Let students know that this average will be used in the next session when students help to advise the Rosadas on a single price for any combination.

Journal Writing

Ask students to think about uses of averages and make a list of where averages are used. Have students explain the importance of one of those averages and how it is used.

See the "Behind the Scenes" section on page 89 for more information on statistics.

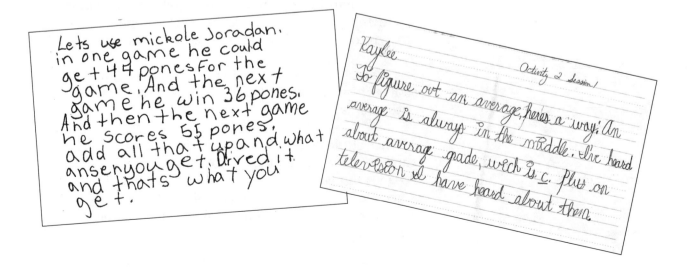

Session 2: Setting the Price

Restaurant Pricing

1. Let students know that in the restaurant business, owners need to charge more than the cost of the ingredients. Ask why they think that is. [To cover expenses—such as rent, utilities, salaries, and to make a profit.]

2. Likewise, as the Rosadas determine a price for their tostadas, they need to at least triple the ingredient costs to meet their restaurant expenses as well as to make a profit. (Restaurants often use a formula like this, as do other businesses. One general rule of thumb in the restaurant business is to triple the cost of ingredients.)

This provides computational practice in the context of solving a problem.

3. Put the Tostada Cost Chart transparency on the overhead. Have students triple the cost of each combination.

4. Circulate as they work. When they finish calculating, have the class come to consensus on the cost for each combination after it is tripled. Record the tripled costs on the overhead below the Total Cost.

Quote A Price!

1. As your students know, the Rosada family wants to set one standard price for all of their tostadas. The Rosadas have determined that they sell almost an equal number of each combination every day.

2. Have students work with their partners to determine a single price to recommend to the Rosadas. They need to have a convincing argument as to why it is the best price. Tell them to be sure to include numbers, comparisons, and any type of data analysis in their explanations.

3. As students are working, circulate to observe their strategies and the tools that they use. Answer and ask questions as appropriate.

4. When students are done, refocus the class and have partners make a case for the price that they think the Rosadas should charge. Ask questions that help students articulate their methods for determining the price and encourage students to likewise ask questions of their classmates.

Journal Writing

Have students write a convincing argument in the form of a persuasive letter to advocate their price for the Rosada's tostada combinations. Ask them to be sure they include their data analysis and an explanation of how they determined the price. Students can include factors such as discounts for large families.

Going Further

1. Class Averages. Determine the average for other measurements related to students, such as head size, foot length, arm length, arm span, leg length, etc. Are there any relationships among the different body measures? Students can use lengths of string or measuring tape to take the measurements.

2. Athletic Averages. Have students determine the class average for such activities as: broad jump, number of basketball shots made in a certain number of minutes, number of jumps jumping rope, running time in 50 yd. dash, etc. Students can help generate ideas for this.

3. Family Averages. If appropriate, collect data about aspects of the students' families to determine averages for the class. For example, find the average number of children in each family or the number of pets.

4. Consumer Research. Have students go the store with their families to find out the actual costs of the ingredients for tostadas. Compare the store prices to the prices used in the activity. As they record items, have students include the weight, volume, or quantity of each item and the number of servings. Calculate the cost of a serving size using the serving size on the package.

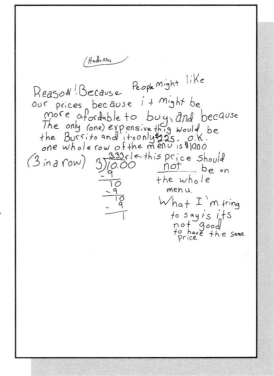

5. This activity combines aspects of what students learned in Activities 1 and 2. It can also serve as an assessment (see "Assessment Suggestions," page 112).

Sandwich Shop. The Clinkscales family went to a sandwich shop for lunch. The shop makes combination sandwiches from the following choices of ingredients: ham, turkey, salami, cheddar cheese, and Swiss cheese. Sandwiches include lettuce and tomato at no extra charge.

a. **Two Choices**—Each family member chooses *two* of these ingredients (meat and/or cheese) on their sandwiches. For example: Cloud chose turkey and Swiss cheese. How many different combinations with two ingredients do they have to choose from? Have students explain their answer and be sure to use charts, pictures, diagrams, or any other tools to help illustrate the solution. Have them explain why they are certain there are no other choices.

b. **Add Avocado**—If the sandwich shop offers avocado as another choice on their sandwiches, how will that change the number of possible combinations? Have students explain their answer.

c. **Sandwich Pricing**—The sandwich shop charges depending on the items selected for the sandwich. The prices are: $1.25 for ham; $1.15 for turkey; $1.00 for salami; $1.10 for cheddar cheese; and $1.20 for Swiss cheese. With two items per sandwich, what is the most expensive sandwich? What is the least expensive? What is the average price for a sandwich? If the shop owners were going to charge one standard price for any two-choice combination sandwich, what price would your students recommend? Have them explain how they arrived at this price and why they think it is the best.

6. This activity combines aspects of what students learned in Activity 2. It can also serve as an assessment (see "Assessment Suggestions," page 112).

Recycling. Discuss the environmental benefits of recycling and what type of recycling is done in your area. Have students choose a recyclable item to gather data on, such as aluminum cans.

a. Weekly Average—Have each student keep track of how many aluminum cans their family recycles for one week, and determine the average number of cans used by each person in the household. Record the total number of cans each student's family recycles for the week on a chart. Have students organize the data to determine the range and calculate the average. Are there any modes? If so, compare the average to the mode.

b. More Data—Have students collect data on aluminum cans for another week. How does the number of cans this week compare to the number from the previous week? Students should determine the average number of cans their family recycled in two weeks and the average number of cans recycled by each family member. Record the average number of cans recycled by each family for two weeks. Have students organize the data to determine the range and calculate the average. Are there any modes? If so, compare the average to the mode. Compare the data from week one and week two.

Michelle
4-23-98
Math

How I found the average is: I added all 10 of the prices together, and what ever it added up to, I would devide it by ten, because there was 10 prices and what ever number that was the anser to the devision thing was the anser to the whole thing.

1. jumprope
2 sports
3. reportcards
4. Math

Name Marisa grade 3rd Mrs. Maro
5-7-98
Math Journal

A prophit
Let's say you buy something for 6 dollars! OK and you got tired of it so you wanted to sell it at a garge sale at your house. But if you sell it for the same price you wan't get any money so you would have to double it to get some money from custumer Today we studied prophits and I like the Idea how people double it at a restraunt or else they would not make any mony! If I worked at a restraunt I'd be happy to triple it! And I'd get my money and the people would get there food!

TOSTADA INGREDIENT COSTS

OLiVES _____ ¢

LETTUCE _____ ¢

SALSA _____ ¢

CHEESE _____ ¢

BEANS _____ ¢

TORTiLLA _____ ¢

TOSTADA COST CHART

OLIVES ____ ¢										
LETTUCE ____ ¢										
SALSA ____ ¢										
CHEESE ____ ¢										
BEANS ____ ¢										
TORTILLA ____ ¢										
TOTAL COST										

Activity 3: *Combination Plates*

Overview

In Activity 3, students apply what they have learned about combinations to solve a new problem. With the success of tostadas at the *La Tostada Sabrosa* Restaurant, the Rosadas have decided to expand their menu. In addition to their famous tostadas, the bill of fare now includes the following Mexican dishes: tamales, chiles rellenos, enchiladas, tacos, quesadillas, and burritos. The Rosadas will feature combination plates of these Mexican foods. The combination plates are chosen from the six items, and each item on the plate must be different. In this activity, the Rosada family wants to know how many different combinations are possible given the six food choices. After these are determined, your students are given an "allowance" to select the combination plate of their choice.

In Session 1, "Making Combo Plates!," there are two possible pathways depending upon your assessment of your students' understanding of combinations. In both cases, the Rosada's children suggest answers to the number of combination plates possible with the expanded menu. In one case, their son, Joaquin says that there are 12 possible combination plates, if customers can choose any **two** different items on their plates. In the other case, their daughter, Juanita says that there are 18 possible combination plates, if customers can choose any **three** different items on their plates. **One** of these solutions is presented to the class, and then *independently*, students write a response to **Joaquin's or Juanita's** solution that explains why they agree or disagree with the solution to the combination plate problem.

After writing their responses, students work with a partner to determine the number of combinations possible. They are given free rein to decide what tools they will use to solve the problem. Their solutions are shared and discussed. This provides opportunities to see multiple approaches and solutions to the problem, and fosters classroom discourse. At the end of their discussion, students have time to reflect on what they have learned and again write in their journals. They are also given a new problem to solve for homework that will provide further insights into their understanding of combinations.

Your student's journal writing from Activity 1 will help inform you about which solution is most appropriate for your students.

For many third graders and students who are working with combinations for the first time, Joaquin's solution provides an appropriate next challenge.

By giving students a solution to respond to, you will gain insights into your students' understanding of combinations as well as their strategies to determine the number of combinations for a specific problem.

In Session 2, "Out to Lunch," your students are given an allowance to spend at the Rosada's restaurant. They can choose either a two or three combination plate **depending upon which problem they did in Session 1.** Those that did Joaquin's combinatorial problem will have a choice of two items and those that did Juanita's combinatorial problem will have a choice of three items. Prices are posted for the food items available. First, students calculate the cost of each combination plate to determine if they can select any combination given their set budget. When they know the choices available within the budget, they choose the combination plate they would like. After all students have made their selections, the class can determine how much the class bill would be if they actually went to the restaurant!

This activity gives students continued experience with combinations, providing many opportunities for students to apply what they've learned and to acquire new strategies and tools for solving similar problems. In addition, they practice number skills as they calculate the cost of combination plates. Students work both cooperatively and independently which provides different ways to assess their understanding.

What You Need

For the class:
- ❏ 1 overhead transparency of Joaquin's Solution (master on page 53)

    OR
- ❏ 1 overhead transparency of Juanita's Solution (master on page 54)
- ❏ 1 overhead transparency of the Combination Plate Menu (master on page 55)
- ❏ 1 overhead transparency of either Joaquin's **OR** Juanita's Solution Combination Chart (masters on pages 56 and 57)—depending on the problem students do in Session 1
- ❏ blank overhead transparencies
- ❏ overhead pens
- ❏ an overhead projector
- ❏ class journals or writing paper
- ❏ a variety of math manipulatives, such as unifix cubes, pattern blocks, tiles, etc.

For each pair of students:
   ❐ 1 copy of the Combination Plate Menu data sheet (master on page 55)
   ❐ 1 copy of either Joaquin's **OR** Juanita's Solution Combination Chart (masters on pages 56 and 57)—depending on the problem students do in Session 1
   ❐ *(optional)* 1 calculator

For each student:
   ❐ 1 copy of either the Designer Cakes **OR** Pizza Combos! homework problem (masters on pages 58–59)

Getting Ready

For Session 1:

1. Decide which opening solution your students will respond to—**either** Joaquin's Solution (combinations of 2 items, master on page 53) **or** Juanita's Solution (combinations of 3 items, master on page 54). Make an overhead transparency of the solution you select as the problem for your class.

Your students' responses to this problem provide an informal assessment of their understanding about combinations.

2. Make an overhead transparency of the Combination Plate Menu (master on page 55).

3. Duplicate one copy of the Combination Plate Menu (master on page 55) for each pair of students.

4. Decide which follow-up problem you will give for homework—either the Designer Cakes (master on page 58) **or** the Pizza Combos! (master on page 59) problem. Duplicate one copy for each student.

5. Provide access to manipulatives, such as unifix cubes, pattern blocks, tiles, or other materials to build physical representations of the combinations.

For Session 2:

1. After using it for Session 1, write the price of each item on the Combination Plate Menu overhead as follows:

Burrito	$2.25	Taco	$1.50
Quesadilla	$1.25	Chile Relleno	$2.00
Enchilada	$1.50	Tamale	$1.75

2. Provide "an allowance" for students as follows:
For students who did Joaquin's problem, provide $3.75.
For students who did Juanita's problem, provide $5.50.

3. Duplicate the Solution Combination Chart (Joaquin's or Juanita's) for the problem your students did in Session 1 to assist them in calculating the costs for each combination plate. Also make an overhead transparency of the appropriate chart.

JOAQUIN'S SOLUTION (2 choices from 6) COMBINATION CHART

BURRITO	X	X	X	X	X										
TACO	X					X	X	X	X						
QUESADILLA		X				X				X	X	X			
CHILE RELLENO			X				X			X			X	X	
ENCHILADA				X				X			X		X		X
TAMALE					X				X			X		X	X

JUANITA'S SOLUTION (3 choices from 6) COMBINATION CHART

BURRITO	X	X	X	X	X	X	X	X	X	X										
TACO	X	X	X	X							X	X	X	X	X	X				
QUESADILLA	X				X	X	X				X	X	X				X	X	X	
CHILE RELLENO		X			X			X	X		X			X	X		X	X		X
ENCHILADA			X			X		X		X		X		X		X	X		X	X
TAMALE				X			X		X	X			X		X	X		X	X	X

Session 1: Making Combo Plates!

Joaquin's Solution (Combination Plates with two choices)

1. Tell your students that the Rosada family has had tremendous success selling tostadas at their restaurant and now they want to expand their menu. They will also feature combination plates with a choice from six Mexican specialties: quesadillas, enchiladas, burritos, tamales, tacos, and chiles rellenos. Put the Combination Plate Menu transparency on the overhead.

2. Tell students that customers can choose **two** *different* items on their combination plates. The Rosada family wants to know how many combinations are possible. Joaquin, who is one of their four children, came up with 12 different combination plates.

3. Put Joaquin's Solution on the overhead and have a student read it to the class. Then, have students write in their journals about why they agree or disagree with Joaquin's solution.

4. When the students are finished, have them share their ideas. Encourage them to ask questions of one another. Expect a range in their responses from those who agree with Joaquin's thinking to those who are accurate in finding the correct number of combinations. You may want to record the different number of combinations that your students generate.

Alternately, you can brainstorm with your students the different types of food prepared in a Mexican restaurant. From their list, decide on six items that the Rosadas will offer in their restaurant.

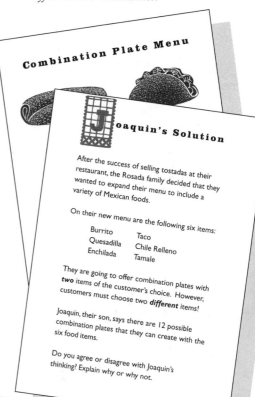

Combination Plate Menu

Joaquin's Solution

After the success of selling tostadas at their restaurant, the Rosada family decided that they wanted to expand their menu to include a variety of Mexican foods.

On their new menu are the following six items:

Burrito	Taco
Quesadilla	Chile Relleno
Enchilada	Tamale

They are going to offer combination plates with **two** items of the customer's choice. However, customers must choose two **different** items!

Joaquin, their son, says there are 12 possible combination plates that they can create with the six food items.

Do you agree or disagree with Joaquin's thinking? Explain why or why not.

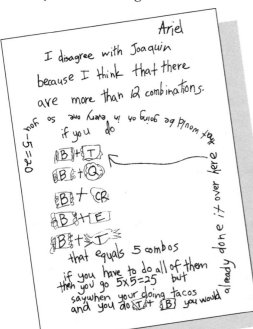

Ariel

I disagree with Joaquin because I think that there are more than 12 combinations.

if you do

B + T
B + Q
B + CR
B + E
B + T

that equals 5 combos

if you have to do all of them then you go 5×5=25 but say when your doing tacos and you do T + B you would already done it over here so you take off every one of it's going to be you so 25-5=20

making combo plates

I agree with Joquain

because 2×6=12 and there are 6 ingretients and you can pick two on a plate

There are 15 possible combination plates. See the "Behind the Scenes" section on page 89 for additional information and ways that the combinations can be organized.

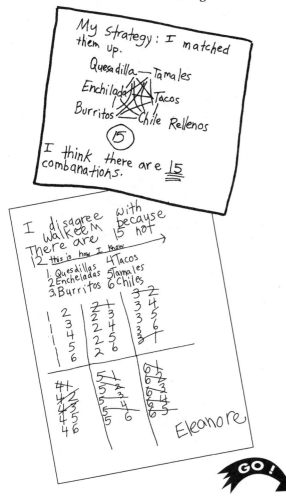

Alternately, you can brainstorm with your students the different types of food prepared in a Mexican restaurant. From their list, decide on six items that the Rosadas will offer in their restaurant.

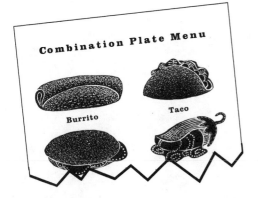

5. In pairs, have students determine and prove how many combination plates there are. Give them free rein to use any materials that will help them. Distribute one copy of the Combination Plate Menu data sheet to each pair of students.

6. Remind students that they will need to prove their thinking to each other. Circulate as students work to gain insight into their problem-solving strategies.

7. When students have completed their work, ask for volunteers to share their solutions. Have each pair of students present their work. Provide time for questions by other students and yourself. Check to see if any other partners had the same or similar solutions.

8. If students share a new organizational strategy, be sure that everyone understands it. As students share their work, there are wonderful teaching opportunities.

Journal Writing

Have students reflect on what they have learned through writing a response to one of the following in their journals:

> Ask students to explain how Joaquin came up with 12 combinations. How would they help Joaquin understand that there are 15 possible combinations?

> What new strategy for organizing the combinations did you learn from listening to other students' solutions?

Juanita's Solution (Combination Plates with three choices)

1. Tell your students that the Rosada family has had tremendous success selling tostadas at their restaurant and now they want to expand their menu. They will also feature combination plates with a choice from six Mexican specialties: quesadillas, enchiladas, burritos, tamales, tacos, and chiles rellenos. Put the Combination Plate Menu transparency on the overhead.

2. Tell students that customers can choose **three** *different* items on their combination plates. The Rosada family wants to know how many combinations are possible. Juanita, who is one of their four children, came up with 18 different combination plates.

3. Put Juanita's Solution on the overhead and have a student read it to the class. Then, have students write in their journals about why they agree or disagree with Juanita's solution.

4. When the students are finished, have them share their ideas. Encourage them to ask questions of one another. Expect a range in their responses from those who agree with Juanita's thinking to those who are accurate in finding the correct number of combinations. You may want to record the different number of combinations that your students generate.

Juanita's Solution

After the success of selling tostadas at their restaurant, the Rosada family decided that they wanted to expand their menu to include a variety of Mexican foods.

On their new menu are the following six items:

Burrito
Quesadilla   Taco
Enchilada   Chile Relleno
                        Tamale

They are going to offer combination plates with **three** items of the customer's choice. However, customers must choose three **different** items!

Juanita, their daughter, says there are 18 possible combination plates that they can create with the six food items.

Do you agree or disagree with Juanita's thinking? Explain why or why not.

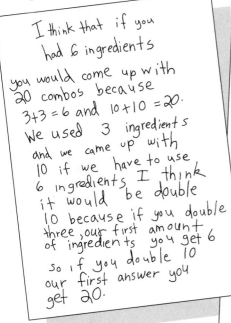

I think that if you had 6 ingredients you would come up with 20 combos because 3+3 = 6 and 10 + 10 = 20. We used 3 ingredients and we came up with 10 if we have to use 6 ingredients I think it would be double 10 because if you double three, our first amount of ingredients you get 6 so if you double 10 our first answer you get 20.

I disagree because last time there were 15 with 2, so if there are combonations of 3 now, and there are 6 choices, then I think you add 6. So that would be (21)

Esther

6⁄2̶1̶
6̶2̶3̶
6̶2̶4̶
6̶2̶5̶
6̶3̶4̶
6̶3̶2̶
6

345   346
356

                246
                245
I disagree
I think that   234
there are 40
or so combos!   235
and I already
have 2!!   236
123   124   125 126
134   135   136
145   146
156

5. In pairs, have students determine and prove how many combination plates there are. Give them free rein to use any materials that will help them. Distribute one copy of the Combination Plate Menu data sheet to each pair of students.

6. Remind students that they will need to prove their thinking to each other. Circulate as students work to gain insight into their problem-solving strategies.

7. When students have completed their work, ask for volunteers to share their solutions. Have each pair of

There are 20 possible combination plates. See the "Behind the Scenes" section on page 89 for additional information and ways that the combinations can be organized.

I agree with 20. Here is how I got the answer

Bur.	Tac.	Tam.	Enc.	Chi.	Que.	
				✓	✓	O 1
		✓		✓	✓	O 2
	✓			✓	✓	O 3
✓				✓	✓	O 4
	✓	✓			✓	O 5
✓		✓			✓	O 6
✓			✓		✓	O 7
	✓	✓			✓	O 8
✓		✓			✓	O 9
✓	✓				✓	O 10
		✓	✓	✓		O 11
	✓	✓	✓			O 12
✓		✓	✓			O 13
	✓	✓	✓			O 14
✓	✓	✓	✓			O 15
✓	✓	✓				O 16
	✓	✓	✓			O 17
✓	✓	✓				O 18
✓	✓	✓				O 19
✓	✓	✓				O 20

Your students' solutions will provide valuable information about their level of understanding. You may want to continue to work on combinations to solidify their understanding. They will have one additional problem involving combinations in Activity 4.

students present their work. Provide time for questions by other students and yourself. Check to see if any other partners had the same or similar solutions.

8. If students share a new organizational strategy, be sure that everyone understands it. As students share their work, there are wonderful teaching opportunities.

Journal Writing

Have students reflect on what they have learned through writing a response to one of the following in their journals:

Ask students to explain how Juanita came up with 18 combinations. How would they help Juanita to understand that there are 20 possible combinations?

What new strategy for organizing the combinations did you learn from listening to other students' solutions?

Homework

The two homework problems are designed to help assess your students' understanding of combinations at this point in the unit. The Designer Cakes problem (page 58) is the same problem as the initial tostada problem in a new context. Students may or may not recognize it as such. The second problem, Pizza Combos! (page 59), also involves combinations, but there are more steps to arrive at a solution. The student data sheets for both problems are at the end of this activity, and the solutions for both are in the "Behind the Scenes" section.

Select the appropriate problem for your students. Provide ample time for them to complete the problem at home. You may want it to be a "Problem of the Week." Be sure to schedule time for students to share their work in class.

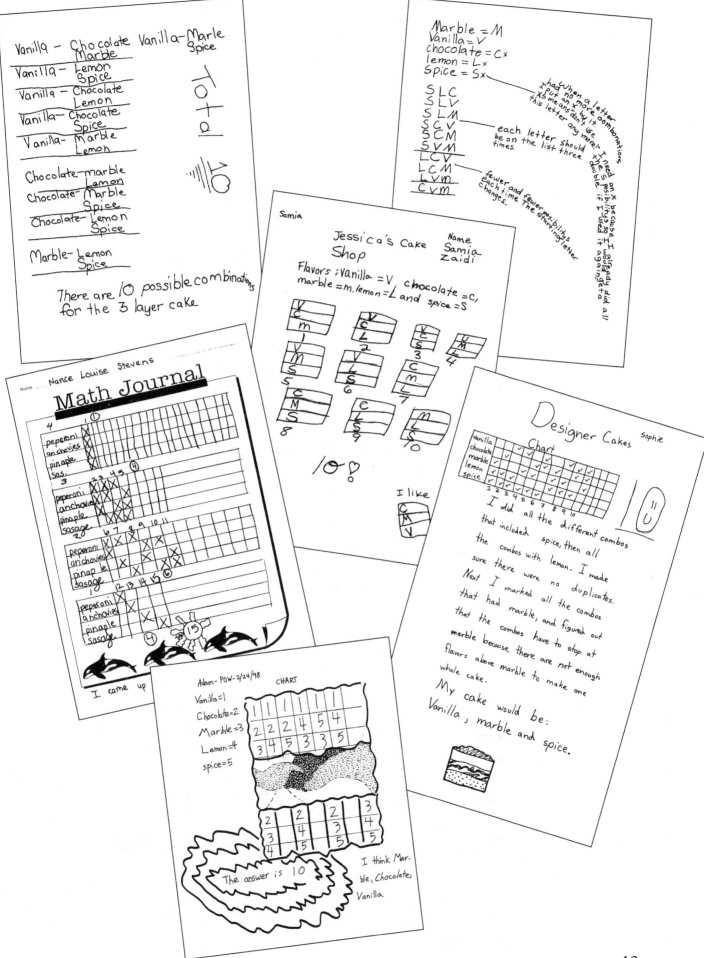

Vanilla – Chocolate Marble   Vanilla – Marble Spice

Vanilla – Lemon Spice

Vanilla – Chocolate Lemon

Vanilla – Chocolate Spice

Vanilla – Marble Lemon

Chocolate – marble Lemon

Chocolate – Marble Spice

Chocolate – Lemon Spice

Marble – Lemon Spice

Total 10

There are 10 possible combinations for the 3 layer cake

Marble = M
Vanilla = V
chocolate = Cx
lemon = Lx
spice = Sx

S L C
S L V
S L M
S C V
S C M
S V M
L C V
L C M
L V m
C V m

When a letter had no more combinations I put an x by it. I need an x because I already did all the S's, the x means don't use this letter any more. it would double if I used it again to a

each letter should be on the list three times.

fewer and fewer possibilities each time the starting letter changes.

Samia

Jessica's Cake Shop   Name Samia Zaidi

Flavors : Vanilla = V chocolate = c, marble = m. lemon = L and spice = S

10 ♡

I like
C
M
V

Name — Nance Louise Stevens

Math Journal

4   ①
peperoni
anchovies
pinaple
sas.

3
peperoni
anchovies
pinaple
sasage

peperoni
anchovies
pinaple
sasage

peperoni
anchovies
pinaple
sasage

15

I came up

Adam - POW - 2/24/98   CHART

Vanilla = 1
Chocolate = 2
Marble = 3
Lemon = 4
spice = 5

The answer is 10

I think Marble, Chocolate, Vanilla

Designer Cakes   Sophie

Vanilla
chocolate
marble   Chart
lemon
spice

I did all the different combos that included spice, then all the combos with lemon. I made sure there were no duplicates. Next I marked all the combos that had marble, and figured out that the combos have to stop at marble because there are not enough flavors above marble to make one whole cake.

My cake would be: Vanilla, marble and spice.

Session 2: Out to Lunch

Depending upon the problem they did in Session 1, they will each have either $3.75 for a two-combination plate or $5.50 for a three-combination plate.

1. Tell your class to pretend that they are going out to lunch at the Rosada's restaurant. Tell them what their allowance is to buy lunch.

2. Put the Combination Plate Menu transparency, which includes the prices, on the overhead. Tell students that the prices include tax.

3. Ask students which combination will be the least expensive. Ask if they can select any combination given the prices.

4. Choose one of the following:

   a. For those students doing the **two** combination plates, distribute Joaquin's Solution Combination Chart or refer students back to their earlier class work on this problem in Session 1.

JOAQUIN'S SOLUTION COMBINATION CHART

	1	2	3	4	5	6	7	8	9	10	11	12	13	14	15
BURRITO	X	X	X	X	X										
TACO	X					X	X	X	X						
QUESADILLA		X				X				X	X	X			
CHILE RELLENO			X				X			X			X	X	
ENCHILADA				X				X			X		X		X
TAMALE					X				X			X		X	X

   b. For those students doing the **three** combination plates, distribute Juanita's Solution Combination Chart or refer students back to their earlier class work on this problem in Session 1.

JUANITA'S SOLUTION COMBINATION CHART

	1	2	3	4	5	6	7	8	9	10	11	12	13	14	15	16	17	18	19	20
BURRITO	X	X	X	X	X	X	X	X	X	X										
TACO	X	X	X	X							X	X	X	X	X	X				
QUESADILLA	X				X	X	X				X	X	X				X	X	X	
CHILE RELLENO		X			X			X	X		X			X	X		X	X		X
ENCHILADA			X			X		X		X		X		X		X	X		X	X
TAMALE				X			X		X	X			X		X	X		X	X	X

5. Have students work with partners to determine how much each combination plate costs to determine which ones they can purchase given their lunch budget.

6. Circulate as students work. Observe how they are working on this problem together. What tools and strategies do they use?

7. When they have finished, ask for the results and record the cost for each combination on the overhead transparency.

8. Have students select the combination plate of their choice and determine if they would receive any change back from their purchase. If so, how much?

9. Continue to ask questions such as: How many combinations can not be purchased? How much more money is needed to purchase them?

10. Have students organize the combination plate costs from the least expensive to most expensive. Ask for their observations about that data. Guide them so that they identify the range in prices, the most commonly occurring prices (modes), and the center of the data (medians).

11. Have students make a graph to represent the classes' choices of combinations. Encourage them to use a variety of graphs to display the same data. Have students calculate the cost of all the combinations they selected to determine the class bill!

Journal Writing

Have students reflect on these activities related to cost by responding to the following problem:

> If the Rosada family wanted to charge a single price for any of their combination plates, what price would you recommend? Why? Explain your thinking and include all the calculations that helped you arrive at your recommendation.

Going Further

1. Restaurant Research. If there are Mexican or Latin-American restaurants in your area, have students help collect menus from those restaurants. Compare the prices of the Rosada's combination plates with another restaurant's prices. Are these prices realistic? If not, how much do the prices need to be adjusted? How do restaurants determine prices to make sure their overhead and other costs are covered and that profit is made?

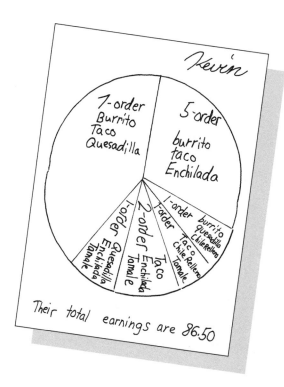

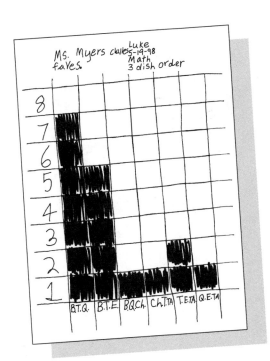

2. Money Sense. To help students understand the value of money, have them work cooperatively to raise money for new materials for the class or for a special field trip. Brainstorm a list of things that they would like for the class or places they would like to go. Take a vote to decide on the top three things on the list. Research the total cost of those three things. Students can make cases for their choice. Vote again to decide which one to purchase or where to go. As a group, discuss fundraising efforts the class can do as well as how students can individually earn money. Get a large money jar and watch the amount grow! This provides the opportunity to see that it takes time and planning to acquire new materials or raise enough money for a special trip. It also gives them a greater appreciation of the materials already in the classroom and the costs behind field trips.

3. Literature Connections. See the "Literature Connections" section for books that connect to Latin foods and traditions including *Day of the Dead*, *Family Pictures*, *Jalapeño Bagels*, and *The Tortilla Factory*. In addition, there are books related to money concepts. In particular, *Pigs Will Be Pigs* focuses on money in the context of going out to eat at the Enchanted Enchilada Restaurant. It includes a menu and money problems to solve, and can be used as a springboard into additional problems.

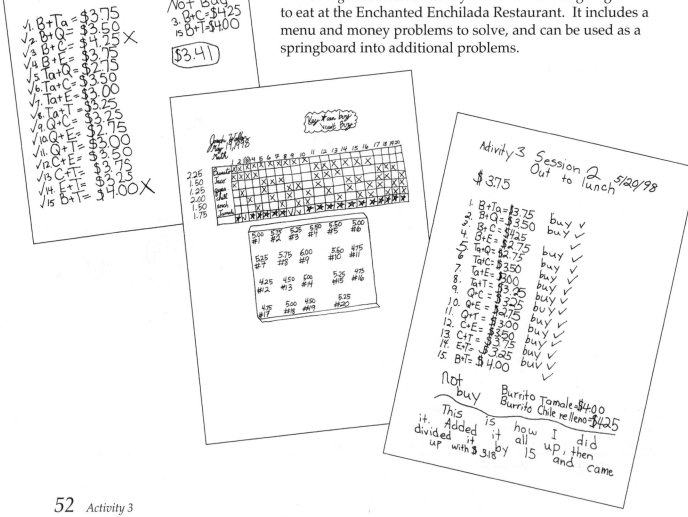

oaquin's Solution

After the success of selling tostadas at their restaurant, the Rosada family decided that they wanted to expand their menu to include a variety of Mexican foods.

On their new menu are the following six items:

Burrito	Taco
Quesadilla	Chile Relleno
Enchilada	Tamale

They are going to offer combination plates with **two** items of the customer's choice. However, customers must choose two **different** items!

Joaquin, their son, says there are 12 possible combination plates that they can create with the six food items.

Do you agree or disagree with Joaquin's thinking? Explain why or why not.

Juanita's Solution

After the success of selling tostadas at their restaurant, the Rosada family decided that they wanted to expand their menu to include a variety of Mexican foods.

On their new menu are the following six items:

Burrito   Taco

Quesadilla   Chile Relleno

Enchilada   Tamale

They are going to offer combination plates with **three** items of the customer's choice. However, customers must choose three **different** items!

Juanita, their daughter, says there are 18 possible combination plates that they can create with the six food items.

Do you agree or disagree with Juanita's thinking? Explain why or why not.

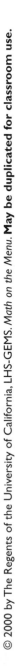

Combination Plate Menu

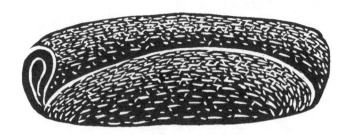

Burrito

Taco

Quesadilla

Chile Relleno

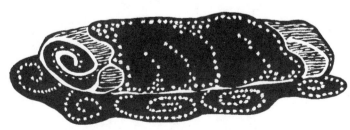

Enchilada

Tamale

Joaquin's Solution

Combination Chart

	1	2	3	4	5	6	7	8	9	10	11	12	13	14	15
BURRITO	X	X	X	X	X										
TACO	X					X	X	X	X						
QUESADILLA		X				X				X	X	X			
CHILE RELLENO			X				X			X			X	X	
ENCHILADA				X				X			X		X		X
TAMALE					X				X			X		X	X

Juanita's Solution

3 choices from 6

Combination Chart

BURRITO	X	X	X	X	X	X	X	X	X	X										
TACO	X	X	X	X							X	X	X	X	X	X				
QUESADILLA	X				X	X	X				X	X	X				X	X	X	
CHILE RELLENO		X			X			X	X		X			X	X		X	X		X
ENCHILADA			X			X		X		X		X		X		X	X		X	X
TAMALE				X			X		X	X			X		X	X		X	X	X

Designer Cakes

A new bakery just opened in town. It features layer cakes made to order. The bakery offers a choice of five different cake flavors: vanilla, chocolate, marble, lemon, and spice.

If you were going to order a three-layer cake, how many different choices can you pick from? Keep in mind that each layer must be a different flavor!

Explain how you determined your solution. Be sure to show all your work including any charts, pictures, and/or diagrams that you use to help determine the answer.

After you determine the total number possible, record the cake of your choice!

Pizza Combos!

You are opening a new pizza shop that features a choice of four special toppings in addition to tomato sauce and cheese.

Customers can choose **any** number of toppings **from one to four.** However, they can not have duplicates of any one topping.

List the four toppings you will offer.

Determine the total number of pizza combinations that can be made at your pizza shop. Hint: Be sure to count *all* the possible combinations of pizzas—one topping, two toppings, three toppings, and four toppings.

Explain how you determined your solution. Be sure to show all of your work, including charts, pictures, and/or diagrams.

Activity 4: La Fiesta Restaurante

Overview

The Rosada family has just purchased a new building on a busy corner in their city to build a larger restaurant—*La Fiesta Restaurante*—that will be able to accommodate up to 46 people. Since they are moving into a brand new building, they are excited about creating a floor plan. The Rosadas already know the dimensions they want for their kitchen and bathroom. They have also purchased a total of 11 tables in three different sizes and 46 chairs.

In Session 1, students work in pairs to become familiar with the restaurant floor plan and paper models of the kitchen, bathroom, and tables. As students explore the limits and possibilities of these items, they become familiar with the dimensions of the kitchen, bathroom, and tables and calculate floor space needed for each item. Next, they are given the building codes for the floor plan. With these parameters in mind, your students become designers to create a floor plan for the Rosadas! When completed, partners present their floor plans to the class and explain the rationale behind them.

In Session 2, students revisit combinations in the context of choosing colors to paint and decorate the new restaurant. As the number of colors the Rosadas select increases, so too does the cost of painting the restaurant! Given their budget, the Rosadas can choose four colors. Initially, there are five colors available, and students determine the number of color combinations possible. Then, the number of color choices increases to six, and again, the Rosadas can only choose four! Using colored cubes, colored paper "paint chips," or another organization tool, students determine the color combination choices for the Rosadas. As students explore this problem, they are applying what they learned about combinations in the earlier activities and deepening their understanding of combinations.

In Session 3, the restaurant is running successfully and parties with more than six people arrive. To accommodate them, the tables need to be situated so they can be easily moved for groups of eight. On a particular Saturday night, the restaurant receives reservations and needs to determine a seating plan, knowing more customers will arrive. Students evaluate their plans and adjust them to accommodate the constraints of the seating problem.

This series of activities related to the Rosada's expanding enterprise interweaves measurement, geometry, number, and discrete mathematics. As students create a floor plan, they use their spatial sense to situate components of varying sizes into the given area. The kitchen, bathroom, and tables are geometric representations of multiplication as is the restaurant grid. They use perimeter and area to solve a problem with a real-world context. Students also apply their understanding of combinations to determine a color scheme for the new restaurant. Throughout the activities, students use numbers in context and work collaboratively.

What You Need

For the class:
- ❐ 1 piece each of 8 ½" x 11" blue and red paper
- ❐ 2 pieces each of 8 ½" x 11" yellow and green paper
- ❐ 1 set of restaurant transparencies (see Getting Ready For Session 1)
- ❐ an overhead projector
- ❐ 1 each blue, red, yellow, and green overhead pen
- ❐ blank overhead transparencies
- ❐ class journals or writing paper
- ❐ *(optional)* 3 pieces each of 8 ½" x 11" blue, red, yellow, green, orange, and purple paper if paper paint color manipulatives are used for Session 2

OR
- ❐ *(optional)* colored cubes in blue, red, yellow, green, orange, and purple

For each pair of students:
- ❐ 1 set of restaurant manipulatives (see Getting Ready For Session 1)
- ❐ 1 small plastic ziplock bag for restaurant manipulatives
- ❐ 3 copies of the Restaurant Floor Plan (master on page 78)
- ❐ 1 copy of the City Building Codes (master on page 79)
- ❐ 1 set of paint color manipulatives (see Getting Ready For Session 2)
- ❐ *(optional)* 1 small plastic ziplock bag for paint color manipulatives

Getting Ready

For Session 1:

1. Prepare student sets of restaurant manipulatives for the floor plan as follows:

   a. Duplicate the Bathroom/El Baño sheet (master on page 75) on blue paper and the Kitchen/La Cocina sheet (master on page 76) on white paper. Cut the duplicated sheets along the dotted lines so that you will have kitchen and bathroom paper manipulatives.

   b. Duplicate the Grid Master (master on page 77) on red, yellow, and green paper. Cut the red grid into 1 x 1 squares, the yellow grid into 1 x 2 rectangles, and the green grid into 1 x 3 rectangles to represent the different sizes of tables in the restaurant.

   c. For each pair of students, place the following items in a ziplock bag:
   - 1 white kitchen/la cocina
   - 1 blue bathroom/el baño
   - 3 red tables
   - 4 yellow tables
   - 4 green tables

You may want to prepare extra kitchens, bathrooms, and tables to supplement sets whose pieces may become lost.

2. For each pair of students, duplicate three copies of the Restaurant Floor Plan (master on page 78) on white paper. The copies will be used as follows: one copy is to use with the paper restaurant manipulatives, one copy is to record a floor plan in Session 1, and one copy is to record another floor plan in Session 3.

3. For each pair of students, duplicate one copy of the City Building Codes (master on page 79).

4. For a demonstration on the overhead, make a set of restaurant transparencies using the masters on pages 80–81. These have been scaled to fit on the overhead projector. Make at least one copy of the Restaurant Floor Plan, the Kitchen, Bathroom, and Tables. To correspond with the paper manipulatives your students use, color the bathroom blue and the tables red, yellow and green using the overhead pens. Both you and your students will use these throughout this activity.

For Session 2:

1. Decide what manipulatives you will make available to assist your students as they solve the paint color combination problem. The following are some possibilities:

- 1" paper squares in blue, red, yellow, green, orange, and purple *(recommended)*; or

- colored cubes (wooden, centimeter, unifix, etc.); or

- paper and pencil

2. If you use paper squares or cubes that correspond to the paint colors, each pair of students needs a minimum of 10 of each color to solve the problem. Rather than provide the exact amount, we recommend 15 of each color. For a class of 32 students, you would need 240 of each color. If you cut 8 ½" x 11" paper into 1" squares, you will get 88 squares per sheet. By cutting 3 sheets of each color, you will have 264 squares.

3. Place the manipulatives in a plastic bag or container to distribute during the activity.

For Session 3:

1. Students again use the Restaurant Floor Plan and paper manipulatives (kitchen, bathroom, and tables) that they used in Session 1.

2. The third copy of the Restaurant Floor Plan that was made for Session 1 is used in this session to record a new floor plan.

Session 1: Designing Floor Plans

Exploring the Floor Space

1. Tell students that the Rosada family has just purchased a new restaurant that is larger than their *La Tostada Sabrosa* restaurant. Since they are moving into a brand new building, they are excited about creating a floor plan. They want to look at a variety of plans before they decide which one to use. They are again asking your students to assist them.

2. Put the Restaurant Floor Plan transparency on the overhead. Tell them the name of the new restaurant and explain what it means—the Party Restaurant.

3. Have students make observations about the floor plan. You are likely to hear some of the following: windows on two sides, a corner entrance with a shaded area, its dimensions (9 squares x 11 squares), the perimeter (40 units) and the area (99 square units).

4. Point out the shaded corner of the restaurant (the doorway). Let students know that these three squares cannot have any objects placed on them (to keep the entryway clear).

5. Distribute one copy of the Restaurant Floor Plan student sheet and one set of the paper restaurant manipulatives to each pair of students.

6. Put the Kitchen overhead on the floor plan. Ask students to determine the dimensions (3 units x 5 units) of the kitchen as well as the perimeter (16 units) and area (15 square units) using their paper kitchen models on the floor plan.

7. Put the Bathroom overhead on the floor plan. Continue by asking students to find the dimensions (2 units x 2 units), perimeter (8 units), and area (4 square units) of the bathroom using their paper models.

8. Tell students that the Rosadas purchased 11 tables as follows—4 tables that seat up to six people, 4 tables that seat up to four people, and 3 tables that seat one or two people.

This is an opportune time to review perimeter and area with your students.

9. Put the Tables overheads on the floor plan. Have students determine the dimensions, perimeter, and area of each table using their paper models. [Green tables: 1 unit x 3 units, 8 units, 3 square units. Yellow tables: 1 unit x 2 units, 6 units, 2 square units. Red tables: 1 unit x 1 unit, 4 units, 1 square unit.]

Enter the Codes

1. Explain that there are city building codes that the Rosadas need to follow in the design of the restaurant. Use the transparencies of the kitchen, bathroom, and tables to illustrate the codes visually as you also explain them. Showing an incorrect placement is a helpful way to make sure that students fully understand the constraints.

2. The kitchen can share one or two sides with the perimeter of the restaurant. It can also stand freely in a location inside the restaurant. Demonstrate the three examples of where it can be situated by sliding the Kitchen overhead pieces to various locations such as:

Slide just one kitchen paper model to the possible locations. Follow the same procedure with the other manipulatives (bathroom and tables).

"LA FiESTA" RESTAURANTE

3. The bathroom must share one or both sides with the perimeter of the restaurant. Ask for a few locations where it can be situated. Demonstrate on overhead with just the bathroom. Where wouldn't you situate it and why?

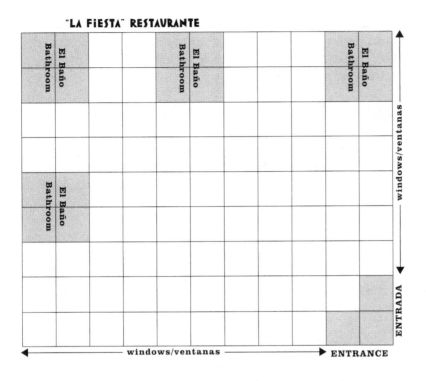

"LA FIESTA" RESTAURANTE

4. Put one transparency of each of the three sizes of tables on the floor plan. Demonstrate how only the shortest side of each table can touch the perimeter of the restaurant along the windows and walls. The tables can also be freestanding with a space around their perimeters.

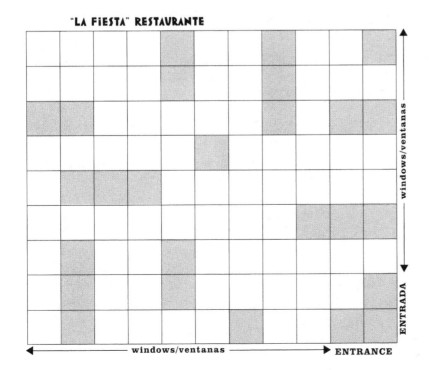

"LA FIESTA" RESTAURANTE

Slide one each of the different tables to various locations.

5. There must be one empty square (or space) between any two objects in the restaurant. This allows for the chairs around the tables and provides space to move around the restaurant.

6. Put a copy of the City Building Codes on the overhead and review the codes. Distribute a copy of the City Building Codes to each pair of students to help them keep in mind the parameters.

Design Time!

1. Tell students that now, working in pairs, they will get to use their paper manipulatives to design a floor plan for the Rosada's new restaurant. As students design their floor plans, circulate to observe them at work.

2. When partners have a plan, have them raise their hands so they can show it to you and explain how their plan meets the city codes. If the plan passes inspection, give them a second Restaurant Floor Plan student sheet to record their plan. If not, have students keep working.

The overheads of the restaurant floor plan, kitchen, bathroom, and tables serve as an important visual tool for students to share their plans.

3. Provide time for students to present their floor plans. Encourage them to explain the strategies they used as they solved the problem as well as the rationale for the final placement of the kitchen, bathroom, and tables.

4. Have students save the paper restaurant manipulatives for Session 3. Post their recorded floor plans. Have students look for similarities and differences in the plans.

Journal Writing

Have students reflect on their process of designing a restaurant floor plan. Use one of the following prompts or create one of your own:

> What strategies did you use to situate the kitchen, bathroom, and tables? Did you have to change and adjust your strategy as you went along? Explain your problem-solving process in detail.

> One trial-test teacher had her students write a persuasive paragraph to the Rosadas explaining why they should choose his or her design over the others. You may want to brainstorm some factors to consider before they begin writing, such as where the kitchen is best situated (in the window, freestanding, against a wall) and why.

Dear La Fiesta,
Thank you for letting us work with you. I think my design is good because the bathroom is out of the way. I like where the kitchen is because when it's in the window people can walk by and stop to look inside the kitchen. They can see what kind of food the restarant has so they can decide if they want to eat there. I like where the tables are because the waiters can get through easily. I also like it because the tables are far apart from each other. It's also good because the tables are near the windows so the can look outside.

Sincerely,
adam
Adam

2/17/00

Dear La Fiesta,
Thank you for leting me do it, it was really fun. I think mine would be a good choice because there would a lot of spuce for the wattes, and the bathroom and the kitcher are out of the wayplus the big tables and kitchen are by the window so that could help advertize and the last thing is the cash-register is on the nearist table so no one could sneek out without paying, thaks agin

Febuary 17, 2000

Dear La Fiesta,
Thanks alot! for letting us have a chance to design your restarount. It was a grand honor. Are plan is wonderful, fasanating, and remarcable. You should chose are plan because:
The party tables are by the windows so people can see people having a good time eating. The bathroom is tucked away so nobody sees it. Family tables (yellow ones) are near the bathroom because, the little kids need to go to the bathroom free quently. The kitchen is in a place ware the waters can go in and out easier. The tables have alot of room inbetween them so the waiter can diliver easier. Hope you chose are plan.

Sincerely,
Kirin Jessel
Kirin Jessel

Dear Lafiesta,
Thank you for coming to parkDay. It was really fun to construct the la fiesta restraunt. I think mine the best because, it has private tables in the back and 1 romantic table in the window. the 2 party tables that are intle window help people see partys eating great food and the kitchen in the window so that people walking by can see the cooks

Session 2: Colorful Combinations

Five Paint Chips

1. Now that the floor plan design has been decided on, the Rosada family is having their restaurant painted before its grand opening. They have consulted with the painters and know that their budget enables them to use four colors.

2. At the initial meeting, the painters brought paint chip samples in five colors—red, green, blue, yellow, and orange. The Rosadas want to know what four-color combinations are possible with these five colors.

3. Have students predict how many combinations they will have to choose from given these five color choices. Provide time for students to discuss the problem with a partner. Have students share predictions and explain the reasoning behind them.

4. Have students work with a partner to determine the number of combinations. Let students know what materials are available to assist them.

5. Circulate as students work. Observe their strategies and listen to their discussions. When students can no longer create unique combinations, focus the class for a group discussion.

6. Ask students how many color combinations the Rosada family has to choose from. Provide time for pairs of students to present their solutions to the class. Depending upon the solutions students present, this may also be an opportune time to demonstrate other organizational strategies to determine the number of combinations.

7. Come to a consensus about the number of combinations that can be proved using a chart (similar to the one used in Activity 1) or another strategy.

Adding One More Choice to the Mix!

1. Tell students the Rosadas wanted to see the color combinations choices if they added one more color choice—purple.

With five color choices to create a combination, there are five possible combinations as follows: RGBY, RGBO, RGYO, RBYO, and GBYO.

2. With six colors available—red, green, yellow, blue, orange, and purple—how many distinct four-color combinations can they choose from?

3. Have students discuss the impact of one additional color on the number of combinations with a partner. How many combinations are possible now? Listen to their predictions. Be sure they explain their thinking.

4. Have partners work on this problem. Circulate as students work. Observe their strategies. Note which students start from scratch, those that build on what they discovered in the previous problem and from discussion, and those that apply new methods.

5. When students can no longer create unique combinations, focus the class for a group discussion. You may get a variety of answers. Again, have students explain their strategies to determine how many combinations there are.

With six color choices to create a combination, there are 15 possible combinations. See "Behind the Scenes" on page 89 for the combinations and more information on combinations.

6. After everyone has presented solutions, review the various strategies to organize combinations.

Journal Writing

Choose one of the questions below or write your own. This reflection serves as an assessment of your students' understanding of combinations as they apply what they learned about combinations from three prior combination problems. Here are two open-ended questions:

What strategy did you use to solve this problem? Explain in detail. Use illustrations, diagrams, and/or pictures to support your explanations.

After solving the problem yourself and also seeing various strategies presented by your classmates to solve this problem, which one do you think is best to use? Explain why.

Session 3: Rave Restaurant Reviews

Big Crowds for Dinner!

1. Tell students that *La Fiesta* has become very popular. The Rosadas have decided to take reservations—especially since some larger groups of people have arrived recently, and their current table set up has made it difficult to accommodate them.

2. Using their paper models of the tables, bathroom, kitchen, and the restaurant floor plan from Session 1, have students arrange the tables so that there is one table for eight, and there are also tables situated close enough together that they could accommodate eight at a moment's notice.

Have students be sure to determine all the table combinations to create tables for eight (6+2, 4+4, 4+2+2).

3. Have partners work on this problem. Circulate and observe how students approach this challenge.

4. Provide time for students to share their strategies and solutions using the Restaurant Floor Plan, Tables, Bathroom, and Kitchen overhead transparencies.

Everybody Loves Saturday Night!

1. Tell students that on a recent Saturday night the Rosadas received the following reservations for 6 p.m. when *La Fiesta* opens:

Braxton	Table for 3
Hosoume	Table for 8
Morales	Table for 4
O'Donohoe	Table for 2
Swanson	Table for 5
Tong	Table for 2
Williams	Table for 4

2. Using their revised floor plans with at least one table for eight from "Big Crowds..." above, have students decide the tables where they would place these customers. They should keep in mind that more people will arrive without reservations and possibly even another party of eight or more!

3. Tell students that beyond creating the floor plan, they will be asked to explain how it meets the needs of the

changing numbers of diners as well as why they think this is the best floor plan.

4. As partners work together on this problem, circulate and observe their strategies. Ask questions to help students who might be challenged by this problem.

5. Distribute the third Restaurant Floor Plan student sheet for students to record their revised plan.

6. Provide time for students to share their strategies and solutions using the overhead transparency models.

Journal Writing

Have students create a problem related to the floor plan for their classmates to solve. They must be able to solve these problems themselves!

Going Further

1. Liven It Up! Ask students—in pairs or individually—to create a mural, tile pattern, or design for a wall in the *La Fiesta Restaurante*. Duplicate their designs so they can be colored in different ways. From a choice of six colors, have students choose four to "paint" their creations. Using a second copy, color the designs with a different combination of four colors. Compare the two designs. Which do they prefer? Why? Try using five colors. An additional challenge for older students is to color the design so that the same color does not "touch" itself.

2. Design A Playground. This activity combines aspects of what students learned in Activity 4. It can also serve as an assessment (see "Assessment Suggestions," page 112). Challenge your students to design a playground, given the following parameters.

A local park has received funding to develop a playground. The dimensions are 75 feet x 100 feet. Since there are children of all ages in the neighborhood, the developers have purchased equipment for a wide age span. This includes:

- a set of swings for young children that requires a 10 x 25 area

- a set of swings for older children that requires a 15 x 30 area

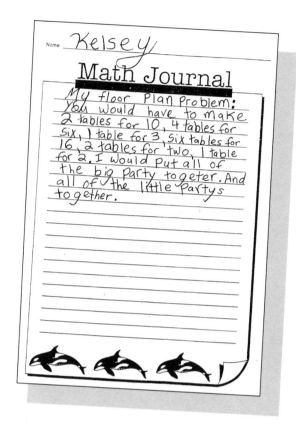

Name Kelsey

Math Journal

My floor Plan Problem: You would have to make 2 tables for 10, 4 tables for six, 1 table for 3, six tables for 16, 2 tables for two, 1 table for 2. I would put all of the big party togeter. And all of the little partys together.

- two separate slides that require a 5 x 12 area and a 10 x 18 area

- two climbing structures that require a 15 x 18 area and a 20 x 25 area

- two picnic tables that each need a 6 x 7 area

- two water fountains that require a 2 x 2 area

Ask your students to design a plan for the park that will serve all the children and also provide a grassy play area. Have students write a letter to the developer explaining why their plan should be selected.

3. Literature Connection. Read the book *Spaghetti and Meatballs for All!* In this humorous story, the seating plan for a family reunion gets very complicated as tables of four are rearranged. In this real-world context, students deepen their understanding of perimeter. The story provides the springboard for other perimeter problems—many of which are included at the back of the book. See "Literature Connections" on page 115.

4. Dream Bedrooms. As a follow up to designing floor plans, one trial test teacher had her students create their ideal bedroom. First, they were given the dimensions of the bedroom and a budget to purchase their furniture. The project involved doing research on the dimensions and cost of the furniture and comparative shopping was encouraged. After the floor plan for the furniture was in place, they were given a second budget to purchase the other things they wanted in their bedrooms. Again, they used real-world prices and did comparative shopping. The grand finale was creating three-dimensional models of their bedrooms.

Bathroom Template

El Baño **Bathroom**	**El Baño** **Bathroom**	**El Baño** **Bathroom**	**El Baño** **Bathroom**
El Baño **Bathroom**	**El Baño** **Bathroom**	**El Baño** **Bathroom**	**El Baño** **Bathroom**
El Baño **Bathroom**	**El Baño** **Bathroom**	**El Baño** **Bathroom**	**El Baño** **Bathroom**
El Baño **Bathroom**	**El Baño** **Bathroom**	**El Baño** **Bathroom**	**El Baño** **Bathroom**
El Baño **Bathroom**	**El Baño** **Bathroom**	**El Baño** **Bathroom**	**El Baño** **Bathroom**
El Baño **Bathroom**	**El Baño** **Bathroom**	**El Baño** **Bathroom**	**El Baño** **Bathroom**

Kitchen Template

... La Cocina ...   ... La Cocina ...   ... La Cocina ...

Kitchen   ... La Cocina ...   Kitchen   ... La Cocina ...   Kitchen   ... La Cocina ...

... Kitchen ...   ... Kitchen ...   ... Kitchen ...

... La Cocina ...   ... La Cocina ...   ... La Cocina ...

Kitchen   ... La Cocina ...   Kitchen   ... La Cocina ...   Kitchen   ... La Cocina ...

... Kitchen ...   ... Kitchen ...   ... Kitchen ...

Grid Master

Restaurant Floor Plan

"LA FIESTA" RESTAURANTE

windows/ventanas

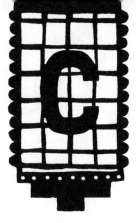

City Building Codes

1. **Kitchen** can:

    a. share 2 sides with the perimeter of the restaurant, **OR**

    b. share 1 side with the perimeter of the restaurant, **OR**

    c. be freestanding within the restaurant.

2. Bathroom *must share* one **OR** both sides with the perimeter of the restaurant.

3. **Tables** can only have their **shortest side** (one unit) touch the perimeter. Tables can also be free-standing.

4. There must be **1 empty square** (or space) between any two objects in the restaurant.

5. Nothing may be placed on the entryway tiles.

"LA FiESTA" RESTAURANTE Restaurant Floor Plan (for overhead)

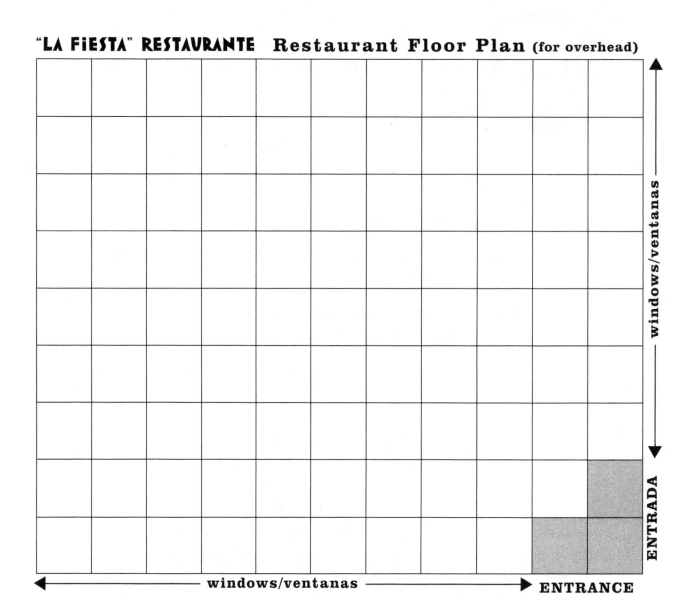

windows/ventanas

ENTRADA

← windows/ventanas → **ENTRANCE**

Kitchen, Bathroom & Tables (for overhead)

Kitchen

Kitchen

La Cocina

La Cocina

**El Baño
Bathroom**

Grid Master

Activity 5: Fiesta Time! *(Optional)*

Overview

After working on the mathematical explorations related to food and restaurants in this unit, your class is sure to enjoy a food fiesta of their own. This can take many forms from a "make your own tostada" party to a potluck of favorite Mexican foods. This celebration can be just for your class, or you may want to include the families of your students as well. **While we realize that such a gathering may not prove practical in all situations, we heartily recommend it as a satisfying finale to this unit!**

As you plan the fiesta of your choice, there are many mathematical investigations intrinsic to the preparations. Students can help determine the quantity of food needed and the costs involved. In addition, they will need to plan for paper goods on which to serve the food, as well as utensils and serving dishes. If the celebration includes their families, students will need to determine the total number of people who will attend. Then, as in Activity 4, they will need to be sure there is enough seating to accommodate everyone!

Due to the open-ended nature of this activity, there are no specific directions for materials to purchase or how to get ready. Instead, a few possible fiestas are described, with ideas for student activities to accompany them. Choose one of these or create one of your own! We would love to hear about what you do!

On the day of the party, you may want to bring in Mexican or other Latin-American music to add to the festivities. You could encourage students—especially any Latin-American students—to share aspects of these rich and diverse cultures.

Be sure that your students have an opportunity to share their work from this unit with their families. At a fiesta or on a designated day, you many want to set up centers with the activities from the unit for parents to do with their children.

Fiestas

Tostada Fiesta For Your Class ONLY!

• First, students need to determine the toppings they want on their tostadas. As a class, make a list of all of their suggested toppings. Take a survey to create a graph or tally of topping preferences of all students. Based on the results, the class decides on the toppings.

• Next, determine the number of toppings allowed on each tostada. Have students decide on the combination they want and record it. Have students determine the total number of people who want each topping.

• Based on the number of people who want each topping, students can determine the quantity of each topping to purchase. This will involve some grocery store research. Assign a food item to teams of students. Be sure one group also researches the cost of the fried tortillas—the tostada base! Working independently the students need to find out the various packaging sizes the topping is sold in, what a serving size is, and the costs of that topping. Encourage students to find out this information for at least two different brands of their topping. This is best done as a homework assignment over the course of a week.

• After researching independently, students share their research information with team members. As a group, they can determine an average serving size for the topping. Based on the number of people who want that topping, they will know the total quantity needed for the class. Given the cost of the topping and the quantity needed, they can determine how much money that topping will cost in total for the class.

• When all the groups determine the cost of their individual toppings, determine the total cost for all toppings and tortillas. Ask how the cost for all the food for the party can be paid for. Listen to their ideas. Solutions can vary from each student contributing an equal amount of money to each student bringing in some of the food.

• You may want to include other expenses, such as paper plates, napkins, utensils, and serving dishes, during the research on toppings. Alternately, you may want to provide these for your students. In addition, you may want to consider having a beverage to accompany the tostadas. Again, this could be part of the research that students do before they determine the total cost.

Tostada Fiesta For Your Class and Their Families

• If you want to include families in a tostada celebration, you can follow a similar procedure as before. The class would start in the same way and determine the toppings that would be available. Then students would survey their families about what toppings they would want. The grand totals would be used to determine how much to buy. In addition, students would have to determine the room(s) in which to hold the party and make sure there is adequate seating to accommodate everyone.

• Alternately, you could arrange a more informal tostada party. Brainstorm with your students toppings that they would like on their tostadas. Determine what toppings are the most popular and approximately how many students should bring each topping. Ask parents to help their children prepare the assigned topping. Tell them that the topping needs to serve a certain number of people. Instead of toppings, have some students and their families contribute tostada shells, paper goods, or beverages. Again, students would determine where to hold the party and make sure there is adequate seating to accommodate everyone.

Combination Plate Fiestas

• This type of fiesta lends itself to a potluck meal and serves as a unifying way for your students' families to get together. Students would survey their families' availability to attend the potluck on a designated evening and report back on the total number of family members who could attend. Once a date is established, students add up the total number of people who can attend.

• Based on the number of people attending, students would determine how many dishes that serve eight people are needed.

• In addition to foods like enchiladas and tacos, you may want to include rice, beans, salad, and tortillas as items to prepare for the meal. This meal also requires beverages, paper goods, and utensils. You may have to decide how to allocate the assignments for food and serving materials. Students can determine the room(s) in which to hold the party and make sure that there is adequate seating to accommodate everyone.

Have a great time!

Going Further (for the whole unit)

1. Order Counts! The **order** in which the combination is placed on a tostada can be important. For instance, the following combination beans, cheese, and salsa can be placed on a tortilla six different ways! (BCS, BSC, CBS, CSB, SBC, SCB) These six variations on the combination are called *permutations.* Have your students determine all the permutations for the tostada combinations! (See "Behind the Scenes" for more on combinations and permutations.)

2. Permutations in Literature. Continue to stretch your students' thinking by reading *Anno's Three Little Pigs* by Mitsumasa Anno and Tuyosi Mori which visually illustrates permutations in a clear format. See the "Literature Connections" section on page 115.

3. Multicultural Foods. Investigate foods that are part of many cultures, such as bread and rice. The book *Bread, Bread, Bread* by Ann Morris is filled with photographs of the different types of bread worldwide as well as the people who eat them! The book *Everybody Cooks Rice* by Norah Dooley takes place in a diverse neighborhood where the reader is introduced to families of many cultures who prepare rice in a variety of ways. Recipes are included. For more about these books, see the "Literature Connections" section on page 115.

4. Present students with the following combination problem, which can also serve as an assessment (see "Assessment Suggestions," page 112):

Combo Cats. C.J. is learning about cats at school. He found out that cats have an excellent sense of hearing and their ears are one of two shapes—rounded or pointed. He also was surprised to discover that some cats have short tails, although most have long tails to help with balance.

> **a. Ears and Tails**—How many different cats can C.J. draw with different ears and tails? Have students explain their answer and be sure to use charts, pictures, or diagrams to illustrate the solution. Students should explain why they are certain there are no other cats with combinations of these two characteristics.
>
> **b. Add Coloration**—C.J. also found out that cats have different coloration and markings for protection. Some cats are solid in color, others have stripes or spots. Without thinking about the different colors themselves—just the markings—

how many cats can C.J. draw using the following characteristics, with one choice allowed for each: coloration—solid or stripes or spots; ears—pointed or rounded; tail length—short or long. Have students explain their answers, use charts, pictures, or diagrams to help illustrate their solutions, and explain why they are certain there are no other cats with combinations of these characteristics.

5. Video Connection. Two videos can be used as instructional tools during or after the unit. A few important things to insure the benefits of videos in the classroom: *preview* the video and decide what segment(s) you want to show; *create an environment* for active viewing; use techniques to keep *students focused and involved* (view only one segment, pause and discuss or predict, turn off sound, show second time, etc.); provide a *follow-up* activity.

a. Eddie in Barbieland. From *The Eddie Files* series that feature Eddie, an 11-year-old East Harlem student in Mrs. Toliver's class, viewers are taken from his classroom into the world outside, where they meet people in real jobs. This particular episode (which runs 22 minutes) is about combinations and the counting principle. Mrs. Toliver poses the first problem and multiple solutions are shown. As they venture out into the world, they meet a Barbie™ fashion designer, an advertiser/marketer, and a Hot Wheels™ designer. In each case, they talk about the mathematics they use in their jobs. Designed for grades 3–6. For information on how to acquire this video, visit
http://shop2.pbs.org/pbsvideo/default.asp

b. Let Me Count the Ways: Counting with Combinatorics. This video is from the *Math Talk* series and emphasizes problem-solving, reasoning and math communication. The cartoon hosts are Maria Lopez and Buster, a parrot, and each episode also includes real-world characters. In this episode (which runs 13.5 minutes), combinations of clothes are the first problem. Next, a variation of this problem is posed on the game show embedded in the show called, "The Square One Challenge." Instead of finding the number of outfits, the challenge is to determine the minimum number of shorts needed to make 20 outfits given 6 shirts. The final problem involves combinations using three toppings that can be put on an ice cream cone. Designed for grades 4–6. For information on how to acquire this video, contact
GPN
P.O. Box 80669
Lincoln, NE 68501
(800) 228-4630

Behind the Scenes

The following information is provided for teachers as mathematical background for this unit, with discussion of several major mathematics strands interwoven in this unit: Discourse; Discrete Mathematics; Data Analysis and Statistics. This information is not intended to be read out loud to students or duplicated for them to read. Following this mathematical background, there is a brief background section on the tortilla. See "Resources" and "Literature Connections" for many more pathways to the cultural connections that could be made to this unit.

Discourse

Discourse is the way knowledge is constructed and exchanged in the classroom. Both the teacher and the students play important roles in shaping the discourse. Above all, mathematical discourse is focused on making sense of mathematical ideas and using those ideas sensibly to set up and solve problems.

Teachers serve as skillful facilitators who orchestrate the communication and learning of mathematics by posing questions, listening carefully to students' ideas, guiding discussions, allowing students to grapple with problems, providing content, monitoring participation of all students, as well as being skillful at which interventions (if any) to use and when.

Students are active participants in their learning working both collaboratively and independently. They have access to a variety of tools to solve problems and present solutions. Students also make conjectures and try to convince one another of the validity of representations, solutions, conjectures, and answers. They rely on mathematical evidence and arguments to determine validity.

The classroom environment is a major influence on what students learn in mathematics. For discourse to flourish, the environment needs to support open dialogue and engage all students in mathematical thinking and learning. Students are the audience for one another. To enhance discourse, the teacher encourages the use of concrete materials as models; pictures, diagrams, tables, and graphs; invented and conventional terms and symbols; written and oral hypotheses, explanations and arguments; and technology tools.

Throughout this guide, discourse is used to introduce and develop mathematical ideas. Students actively construct

Additional information on mathematical discourse with examples of discourse in action can be found in the Professional Standards for Teaching Mathematics (see "Resources" on page 110).

understanding of concepts—from the concrete to the connections and abstract levels—through activities that build on prior knowledge. Multiple solutions provide a broadening of problem-solving strategies as well as new tools to apply when encountering similar problems. The teacher serves as the facilitator encouraging students and providing information, tools, and questions at strategic points during classroom discourse.

Discrete Mathematics

Discrete mathematics is used in the real world in many arenas including scheduling delivery routes, organizing tournament schedules, marketing strategies, computer programming, apportionment of seats in Congress, and mortgages. Discrete mathematics includes set theory (Venn diagrams, union), combinatorial mathematics (permutations, combinations), graph theory (graphs, networks), and recurrence relations and iterations (sequences).

The term discrete emphasizes a countable number. This "countable number" is often arranged in sets, in arrays, or other types of diagrams. Discrete mathematics focuses on separate, rather than continuous qualities. To illustrate this, consider the following real-world examples of discrete items versus those that are continuous:

Discrete	Continuous
Sugar Cubes	Honey
Peas and Carrots	Mashed Potatoes
Hopping rabbit	Slithering snake
Climbing up stairs	Going down a slide

In each of these examples, the discrete items are readily countable, whereas the others are continuous measures and much harder to differentiate in a separated fashion.

Mathematical models are useful tools when working on discrete mathematics problems. For example, charts or diagrams that list the finite, countable number of outcomes to probability problems are tools to determine the theoretical probability. Similarly, charts and diagrams can be used to determine the number of combinations or permutations to a combinatorics problem. Venn diagrams illustrate the ways that groups of objects are both separate from each other and have some attributes in common (intersect). Networks can be drawn to determine if they can be traveled, and furthermore, if they can, whether they are paths or circuits. Graph theory uses diagrams to solve problems, such as the fewest number of zoo habitats needed for a given number of animals.

Combinatorics

Combinatorics includes **combinations** and **permutations.** Students from primary grades through high school explore combinatorial mathematics at their appropriate levels. The activities in this guide are designed for third through fifth grade students and develop an understanding of combinations that can be taken to a deeper and more abstract level at later grades.

As a basis for developing understanding about the combinatorial mathematics in this unit, here are two definitions:

A **combination** is a selection of a set of objects irrespective of the order in which they are chosen.

A **permutation** is an arrangement of a set of objects in a definite order.

To bring these definitions to life, consider a **real-world example.** You are in an ice cream store that sells two-scoop cones of ice cream. There are three flavors to choose from—vanilla, chocolate, and strawberry. You must choose two different flavors on your cone selection. How many different choices of ice cream cones do you have?

Looking at just the **combinations** of flavors, here are the possible solutions:

In this case, the set of objects is three flavors of ice cream. Each flavor can be paired with two other flavors. There are only 3 possible combinations, since we are NOT taking the order of the scoops into account! There is a finite number of objects, which when arranged in this organized manner, represent the solution—the three different cones there are to choose from.

Now, IF the ORDER of the flavors on the cone is taken into consideration, the problem changes so that more arrangements of the ice cream scoops can be created. The following are the six ways the three flavors can be arranged with order taken into consideration:

Again, the set of objects to arrange is the three flavors of ice cream. However, this time there are 6 possible **permutations,** because we are taking the order of the scoops into account. Each of the 3 combinations from above can be arranged in a new way!

Combinations in *Math on the Menu*
In this guide, students have many opportunities to solve **combination problems.** With each new problem they solve, students apply what was learned and deepen their understanding of combinations. In addition, they gain insights into the various strategies and tools to assist them in solving combination problems.

Students have the opportunity to use concrete materials—such as paper models of tostadas, blocks, and paint chips—to help them determine the possible combinations given a set of objects. From the concrete materials, they learn how to use charts, diagrams, and pictures to illustrate their solutions as well as symbolic representations. These tools are used to help explain, communicate, and prove solutions to the various problems.

The solutions for each of the combinations problems follows below. In some cases, the only solution displayed will be in chart form. **Do not feel limited to this one organizational system.** Your students may also come up with other ways to display their solutions. This gives you valuable information on their problem solving strategies and prior knowledge.

In Activity 1, **Tasty Tostadas,** students are given a choice of five toppings for tostadas and are asked to determine how many tostada combinations can be made if only three different toppings could be chosen from the five. Order is not mentioned! In this problem, order is NOT meant to be taken into account. If your students ask about it, steer them back to just looking at combinations initially. (Later in the unit, they are asked to determine how many are possible if order *is* taken into account.) Here is a chart to illustrate the solution:

Tostada Combination Chart

10 possible tostadas with 3 different toppings chosen from 5 toppings

OLIVES			X		X	X		X	X	X
LETTUCE		X		X		X	X		X	X
SALSA	X			X	X		X	X		X
CHEESE	X	X	X				X	X	X	
BEANS	X	X	X	X	X	X				

It can also be arranged as follows:

BEANS	X	X	X	X	X	X				
CHEESE	X	X	X				X	X	X	
SALSA	X			X	X		X	X		X
LETTUCE		X		X		X	X		X	X
OLIVES			X		X	X		X	X	X

In each case, the chart is systematically filled in with "Xs" to record possible combinations. In the first chart, the orientation is from bottom to top whereas in the second chart, there is a top to bottom organization. In both cases, the combinations start with beans and all the possible combinations that can be made using beans are recorded. Next, the combinations that can be made with cheese are recorded **without** repeating the ones that include beans. The chart continues by taking the next ingredient salsa for which there is only one new combination. Check the chart for the other combinations that use salsa. They have already been included in the other combinations! Likewise, for lettuce and olives, the combinations are already created for each of those ingredients.

These are not the only two ways to fill the chart. Students have come up with many other ways to systematically chart the ten combinations. As your students share their methods, be sure that their thinking makes sense and the class understands it. Pose questions to have students clarify their thinking.

In addition to the chart, there are other ways to organize the combinations. One way is to represent the food items symbolically with numbers or letters as follows:

Numbers		**Letters**	
Beans	= 1	Beans	= B
Cheese	= 2	Cheese	= C
Salsa	= 3	Salsa	= S
Lettuce	= 4	Lettuce	= L
Olives	= 5	Olives	= O

The combinations can then be made using numbers or letters as follows:

Numbers	**Letters**
1, 2, 3	B, C, S
1, 2, 4	B, C, L
1, 2, 5	B, C, O
1, 3, 4	B, S, L
1, 3, 5	B, S, O
1, 4, 5	B, L, O
2, 3, 4	C, S, L
2, 3, 5	C, S, O
2, 4, 5	C, L, O
3, 4, 5	S, L, O

Tree diagrams can also be used as a tool to graphically
show the combinations. The following are two examples:

Tree Diagram for Tostada Combination

```
      S                          3
     /                          /
B—C —L                  1—2 —4
     \                          \
      O                          5


      L                          4
B—S <                    1—3 <
      O                          5


B—L—O                    1—4—5


      L                          4
C—S <                    2—3 <
      O                          5


C—L—O                    2—4—5


S—L—O                    3—4—5
```

In Activity 3, **Combination Plates,** students determine the
number of possible combination plates given six food
choices. Again, the order of the food is not taken into
account. Students are also not given specific
manipulatives to use to solve the problem! They are given
a sheet with the six food items to create the possible combinations plates and concrete materials (blocks, cubes, etc.)
are made available.

The students are introduced to the problem with suggested
solutions from one of the Rosada's children—either
Joaquin or Juanita. In each case, they are asked to find the
number of combinations possible.

Joaquin's Solution was given as 12 possible combinations. However, there are in fact **15 possible combinations** given 6 items to create a combination plate each with 2 different foods.

Joaquin's Solution

BURRITO	X	X	X	X	X										
TACO	X					X	X	X	X						
QUESADILLA		X				X				X	X	X			
CHILE RELLENO			X				X			X			X	X	
ENCHILADA				X				X			X		X		X
TAMALE					X				X			X		X	X

Juanita's Solution was given as 18 possible combinations. However, there are in fact **20 possible combinations** given 6 items to create a combination plate each with 3 different foods.

Juanita's Solution

BURRITO	X	X	X	X	X	X	X	X	X	X										
TACO	X	X	X	X							X	X	X	X	X	X				
QUESADILLA	X				X	X	X				X	X	X				X	X	X	
CHILE RELLENO		X			X			X	X		X			X	X		X	X		X
ENCHILADA			X			X		X		X		X		X		X	X		X	X
TAMALE				X			X		X	X			X		X	X		X	X	X

NOTE: Your students may think that Joaquin's and Juanita's solutions were correct because they can apply a multiplication algorithm to it! In the case of Joaquin, given 2 choices from 6 that would mean 6 X 2 = 12 possible combinations. Similarly, Juanita had 3 choices from 6, and 6 X 3 = 18. Your students response to this problem will provide insight into their problem-solving strategies as well as provide information on how they apply what they learned in the tostada problem.

Students may use letters or numbers to represent the food items on the menu and create an organized list. Some students may make tree diagrams for their proofs.

Homework Problems in Activity 3

The homework problems in this activity provide another opportunity for students to solve a combination problem independently or with the help of their family. Students should be able to explain the solutions they bring to school *even if they receive assistance*. Below are charts with the number of combinations possible. Again, other representations of the correct combinations with explanations from your students are not only acceptable, they're also encouraged.

Designer Cakes Combination Chart

There are 10 possible cake combinations with 3 different flavors chosen from 5 flavors.

LEMON	X	X	X	X	X	X				
MARBLE	X	X	X				X	X	X	
CHOCOLATE	X			X	X		X	X		X
VANILLA		X		X		X	X		X	X
SPICE			X		X	X		X	X	X

Pizza Combos! Chart

There are several steps to determine the solution to this problem. Given a choice of 1, 2, 3, **or** 4 choices of toppings, students are asked to find the number of different pizza combinations possible. They need to investigate how many combinations there are for each of the choices: 1 topping, 2 toppings, 3 toppings, and 4 toppings. There are a TOTAL of 15 possible PIZZAS combinations possible as illustrated by the series of charts below that outline the combinations for each number of toppings:

4 Pizzas with only one topping:

Topping A	X			
Topping B		X		
Topping C			X	
Topping D				X

6 Pizzas with two toppings:

Topping **A**	X	X	X			
Topping **B**	X			X	X	
Topping **C**		X		X		X
Topping **D**			X		X	X

4 Pizzas with three toppings:

Topping **A**	X	X	X	
Topping **B**	X	X		X
Topping **C**	X		X	X
Topping **D**		X	X	X

1 Pizza with four toppings:

Topping **A**	X			
Topping **B**	X			
Topping **C**	X			
Topping **D**	X			

From these charts the total number of combinations is:
$$4 + 6 + 4 + 1 = 15$$

In Activity 4, Session 2, **Colorful Combinations,** students determine the possible color combinations that the Rosadas can use to paint their restaurant. The colors can be represented concretely with paper "paint chips," colored cubes, etc. or determined using the organizing tools learned throughout the unit. In the first part of the problem, students are given five choices from which the Rosadas can select four. In the second part, the number of color choices grows to six and again the students determine how many color combinations are possible.

Colorful Combinations Chart

15 possible four-color combinations with 6 colors available

RED	X	X	X	X	X	X	X	X	X	X					
GREEN	X	X	X	X	X	X					X	X	X	X	
YELLOW	X	X	X				X	X	X		X	X	X		X
BLUE	X			X	X		X	X		X	X	X		X	X
ORANGE		X		X		X	X		X	X	X		X	X	X
PURPLE			X		X	X		X	X	X		X	X	X	X

This chart uses a top to bottom organizational system to display the number of possible combinations. There are many other ways to use the chart systematically that also illustrate the combinations.

Other ways to represent the solution include using letters or numbers to represent the colors and create an organized list of combinations, or to use a tree diagram.

If numbers are assigned to the colors like this:

Red = 1 Blue = 4
Green = 2 Orange = 5
Yellow = 3 Purple = 6

Then the 15 possible combinations are:

1, 2, 3, 4	1, 3, 4, 5	2, 3, 4, 5	3, 4, 5, 6
1, 2, 3, 5	1, 3, 4, 6	2, 3, 4, 6	
1, 2, 3, 6	1, 3, 5, 6	2, 3, 5, 6	
1, 2, 4, 5			
1, 2, 4, 6	1, 4, 5, 6	2, 4, 5, 6	
1, 2, 5, 6			

Alternatively, if letters are assigned to the colors like this:

Red = R Blue = B
Green = G Orange = O
Yellow = Y Purple = P

Then the 15 possible combinations are:

R, G, Y, B	R, Y, B, O	G, Y, B, O	Y, B, O, P
R, G, Y, O	R, Y, B, P	G, Y, B, P	
R, G, Y, P	R, Y, O, P	G, Y, O, P	
R, G, B, O			
R, G, B, P	R, B, O, P	G, B, O, P	
R, G, O, P			

As a tree diagram these would be represented in the following ways:

Tree Diagrams:

1—2—3 —5 4 6

R—G—Y —O B P

1—2—4 5 6

R—G—B O P

1—2—5—6

R—G—O—P

1—3—4 5 6

R—Y—B O P

1—3—5—6

R—Y—O—P

1—4—5—6

R—B—O—P

2—3—4 5 6

G—Y—B O P

2—3—5—6

G—Y—O—P

2—4—5—6

G—B—O—P

3—4—5—6

Y—B—O—P

Data Analysis and Statistics

Data and statistics abound from the results of opinion polls regarding the popularity of the President to the amount of rainfall on the weather page of the newspaper. Where does all the information come from and how do we understand it? Statistics are generated in many ways, including surveys, experiments, sports, polls, demographics, and observations.

Statistics involve the collection, classification, analysis, and interpretation of data and are usually represented in graph, table, or chart form. Statistics also include measures of central tendency: mean (average), mode (most frequently occurring number or numbers), and median (number or numbers that fall in the center of the data organized in ascending order). Depending upon what information needs to be conveyed, data can be represented in many different ways. For this reason, data needs carefully analysis to see how the organization impacts its interpretation—in particular, the inferences that can be drawn from it. Being able to interpret and understand statistics is an important life skill—especially in this age of burgeoning technological capabilities that put information at one's fingertips.

In grades three through five, students expand their understanding of data organization and interpretation beyond themselves or what is "the most." They formulate their own questions for investigation and determine how to gather and represent the data. With experience, they can choose the most appropriate method to represent their data from tables to bar graphs, stem-and-leaf plots to circle or line graphs. Finally, students analyze the data to make inferences about what it communicates. There is an emphasis on the use of evidence as validation.

In addition, students gradually develop the concept of an "average" value. To begin, they learn to identify the mode(s) and median(s) in a data set, and then they develop an understanding of what those numbers tell them about the data. Building upon that understanding, they move to the mean (average) which serves as a balance point for the data set.

Data Analysis and Statistics in *Math on the Menu*
In Activity 2, **Money Matters,** students work with data in developmentally appropriate ways. After determining the cost of each tostada combination, they arrange that data

from the lowest to highest number and examine its range. They look for any mode(s) as well as identify the median(s). Next, they calculate the mean. These data are examined to provide experience organizing and interpreting data by looking for central tendencies.

Next, students triple the cost of each combination to reflect real-world economics of restaurants. They are asked to analyze these data to recommend a price to charge for any combination. This takes careful analysis, and rationale must be provided for the price suggested. Students can apply the skills and concepts from the combination cost analysis to this problem.

Students have additional opportunities to solve problems related to data analysis and statistics in the "Going Further" activities in Activity 2. In these activities, students can formulate their own questions for investigation and determine how to gather and represent the data. Students analyze the data to make inferences about what it communicates.

To assess students' understanding of these concepts, the Basketball Stats problem in the Additional Assessment Ideas portion of the "Assessment Suggestions" section (see page 112) can be used. Below is a sample solution to the Chenoa's Points part of the Basketball Stats problem.

Chenoa's Points. In the past twelve games Chenoa has scored the following number of points per game: 23, 19, 25, 20, 17, 24, 16, 27, 21, 24, 22, 26. What is the range of her points per game? Is there a mode(s)? If so, what is it? What is her median number(s) of points? Estimate her average number of points per game and explain how you determined that number. Calculate the average number of points. How close was your estimation to the actual number?

Given Data:
23, 19, 25, 20, 17, 24, 16, 27, 21, 24, 22, 26

Data reorganized from lowest to highest number:
16, 17, 19, 20, 21, 22, 23, 24, 24, 25, 26, 27

Range of points is 11.

Data can also be organized as follows to clearly identify any modes:

24

16, 17, 19, 20, 21, 22, 23, 24, 25, 26, 27

Mode in data set is 24 because it is the only number that occurs more than one time.

Since there is an even number of data, there are two **medians.** Those medians are 22 and 23.

A **stem-and-leaf plot** can also be created to provide another tool to analyze the data.

Chenoa's Points are organized in a **stem-and-leaf plot** as follows:

1| 6, 7, 9
2| 0, 1, 2, 3, 4, 4, 5, 6, 7

Using any or all of the data organizational systems, students can hypothesize about the average (mean) number of points per game. Here is one example of an estimate and the rationale:

"My estimate for Chenoa's average number of points per game is 23. I think this because in 9 of the 12 games she scored at least 20 points and she never scored lower than 16 points. I know her average number of points will be in the 20s because when I organized the data, the median numbers were 22 and 23 and the mode was 24. Since in 5 games she scored 24 or more points, I think it will be 23 points."

"Her average number of points was 22. I estimated only one more than that."

Addressing National Mathematics Standards

The National Council of Teachers of Mathematics (NCTM) is in the process of completing the most current document on mathematics standards, *Principles and Standards for School Mathematics*. In this document, 10 Standards are articulated both in general and by grade level. The activities in *Math on the Menu* address many of the content Standards for grades 3–5 by providing opportunities for students to:

- Calculate averages to determine prices for tostadas, including work with decimals. *Standard 1: Number and Operations*

- Collect, organize, and represent data to determine the average cost of tostada combinations and combination plates. *Standard 5: Data Analysis, Statistics and Probability*

- Interpret data using methods of exploratory analysis to suggest and justify prices for tostadas and combination plates. *Standard 5: Data Analysis, Statistics and Probability*

- Use spatial orientation to create floor plans for a restaurant. *Standard 3: Geometry and Spatial Sense*

- Determine perimeter (in units) and area (in square units) of rectangular shapes as these measurements relate to creating a floor plan. *Standard 4: Measurement*

In addition, the following standards that address how to implement the content are woven throughout the unit and provide the context in which skills and concepts can be learned. In *Math on the Menu*, students:

- Solve problems in a variety of ways using different strategies and apply those strategies to new problems. *Standard 6: Problem Solving*

- Make and investigate conjectures and then use mathematical arguments and proofs to justify findings. (Proving the number of combinations for tostadas, combination plates, and colors for the restaurant.) *Standard 7: Reasoning and Proof*

- Use discourse (see page 89) to communicate mathematical ideas coherently to peers, teachers, and others. *Standard 8: Communication*

- Recognize and make use of connections between different mathematical ideas, as well as between mathematics and contexts outside of mathematics. (Real-world setting of unit with problems involving different content areas.) *Standard 9: Connections*

- Create and use representations to organize, record, and communicate mathematical ideas. (Multiple representations to solve combinatorial problems.) *Standard 10: Representation*

The Story of Corn

The story of the cultivation of corn or maize (*maíz* in Spanish) is a tribute to human connection to the Earth and to the ingenuity of the indigenous peoples of the Americas. Maize cultivation has been traced back many thousands of years and is considered the most remarkable plant breeding accomplishment of all time. Up through to the present, the genetics of maize has fascinated many scientists, including Barbara McClintock, who won a Nobel Prize for her work with maize that led to a breakthrough in understanding the organization and function of genes.

Maize is the domesticated gigantic form of a strain of *teosinte (Zea mays ssp. Parviglumis)* a wild grass now occurring naturally in isolated patches at elevations between 400–1700 meters in the Mexican western Sierra Madre (Michoacan and Jalisco). This small wild grass is the ancestor of today's large ears of corn! Over countless generations, with careful attention to the attributes of each series of plants, native peoples of the Americas developed many wonderful varieties of maize. The biodiversity represented by this careful, scientific cultivation has stood the test of time and greatly enriched the entire world's nourishment.

Early inhabitants of Mexico, Guatemala, and other parts of Mesoamerica were domesticating *maíz* as early as 5000 B.C. Some experts take the original cultivation back even farther. Corn was a major part of the daily diet and spiritual life of the ancient Mayan people, and, as the crop spread to North and South America, of many other tribes and nations. Reverence for corn as the source of life and homage to the Corn Goddess are embedded in Mayan, and later Aztec legends. Peru was home to another civilization built on cultivation of *maíz*. There it was said the god of the earth fires created women and men of glazed clay, breathed life into them, and put ears of corn in the hollow of their right arms, as they began at once to sow the *maíz*. In what is now the northeastern United States and Canada, corn, squash, and beans were known as the "Three Sisters" by native peoples—three sisters who should never be apart and should always be planted together to keep the soil productive.

Interestingly, the cultivation of *maíz* differed greatly from the cultivation of grain in Europe. Indigenous women had a far greater part in the cultivation of *maíz* than European women had in the cultivation of wheat or rye. Also, the

"To most people in the United States, a taco is a tortilla bent in half to form a deep U shape, then fried to a crisp and stuffed to overflowing with ground beef, shredded iceberg lettuce, sliced tomato and grated cheese. Throughout Mexico, however, the simple taco consumed by millions of people daily is a fresh, hot tortilla rolled around some shredded meat or mashed beans and liberally doused with any one of the endless variety of sauces for which Mexico is justly famed, but which are sadly misrepresented this side of the border."

Diana Kennedy
(The Tortilla Book)

Maize agriculture is a powerful example of the co-evolution of a plant and the people who tended it- as the plant and human society evolved, they exerted strong influence on each other. Mexican anthropologist and maize historian Arturo Warman considers maize a cultural artifact, because it is a human invention, a species that does not exist naturally in the wild and can only survive if sown and protected by humans. The domestication and improvement of maize is strongly correlated with the development of cultural complexity and rise of the civilizations of pre-Hispanic Mesoamerica.

indigenous people did not use plows or draft animals. The men prepared the soil with oak poles tipped with metal, and the women sowed the kernels of maíz. The fields were fertilized with ashes from burned wood.

Indigenous peoples also learned that wood ashes could take off the maize kernel's hard-to-digest hull, as could a little lime burned from seashells and limestone. Lime (calcium oxide), which also acts as a preservative, was mixed with the water for cooking corn. The resultant mixture, called *Nixtamal* in the Aztec language, was then ground into dough for making tortillas and other foods. It is still made daily throughout Latin America today, using the same method invented by early peoples.

On the Tortilla

Corn is used in many Latin American dishes, and it is the corn *tortilla* that is the base for many of them. Tortilla is the name given by Spaniards to the corn-based flat-bread they found in use in Mexico. It literally means "smallish and flattened." (Spaniards also call an egg omelette a tortilla.)

It is important to distinguish much of the Mexican food in the U.S. today from the ancient foods of the indigenous Latin American peoples, as well as from authentic Mexican food. Mexican food in the U.S. is increasingly prepared to appeal to the North American palate and is heavy on oils. Too many people only know Mexican food as a crisp, deep-fried taco filled with ground meat heavily flavored with an all-purpose chili powder, and piled high with chopped lettuce.

Nachos, for instance, did not originate in Mexico. The closest thing might be a "totopo" or possibly a "tostada." A totopo is a tortilla made with salt in the dough and baked dry, not pliable. It was made specifically for travelers, as it keeps without spoiling. Tostadas are thin tortillas fried crisp in lard or oil, are often served with refried beans, and with a little *queso fresco* (fresh cheese) crumbled over. A tostada is a post-conquest invention (native cooking before the conquest did not include a number of ingredients/procedures that are now associated with "Mexican food," such as frying, cheeses, etc.). Tostadas are made with a coarser dough than for tortillas. "Chips" are made by shaping this dough and then deep-fat frying it. These oily corn chips devised by big U.S. companies are "nachos."

A taco is comparable to a "sandwich" in that it is made by rolling up any ingredient desired within a corn tortilla—just as anything between two slices of bread is called a sandwich. The greasy "saddle" shell called a hard taco in the U.S. is an industrial creation unknown in Mexico. If instead of a corn tortilla, your "taco" uses a wheat flour tortilla (producing a thick, white flat-bread) then it is called a "burrito." Wheat flour tortillas and burritos are more common in northern Mexico and not generally favored in central/southern Mexico, where corn rules. If you ask for a "burrito" in the south, it might even be thought you were asking for a four-legged animal!

Corn is only one of many crops contributed by pre-Columbian peoples in Latin America to modern diets around the world. Research suggests that the world owes roughly half the items of our present-day food supply to the achievements of ancient indigenous plant breeders in the New World. For lots more on corn and related matters, we recommend the Internet, including:

Corn in the Classroom Home Page:
http://www.ontariocorn.org/citc.html

The Maize Page:
http://www.ag.iastate.edu/departments/agronomy/cornpage.html

In the United States, there is a trend away from corn tortillas to tortillas made with flour. The Aztecs were known to have white flour (from the amaranth plant), but it was not made into tortillas. It is only in the flat, irrigated land in the northern Mexican states of Sinaloa and Sonora that wheat is grown and used for tortillas de harina de trigo. The wheat-flour tortilla in Mexico resulted from European introduction of wheat there and is probably based on imitation of the corn version. It is similar to Mediterranean flat-breads, such as "pita" bread and has come to be known as "pan Arabe."

BIBLIOGRAPHY

Atkinson, Sonja, *The Aztec Way to Healthy Eating*, Paragon House, New York, 1991.

Bayless, Rick with Deann Groen Bayless, *Authentic Mexican: Regional Cooking from the Heart of Mexico*, William Morrow, New York, 1987.

Gerlach, Nancy and Jeffrey, *Foods of the Maya: A Taste of the Yucatán*, The Crossing Press, Freedom, California, 1994.

Jacob, H. E., *Six Thousand Years of Bread: Its Holy and Unholy History*, The Lyons Press, New York, 1944.

Kennedy, Diana, *The Cuisines of Mexico*, Harper & Row, New York, 1972.

Kennedy, Diana, *The Tortilla Book*, Harper & Row, New York, 1975.

Leonard, Jonathan Norton, et al., *Latin American Cooking*, Time-Life Books, New York, 1968.

Sources

Base 10 Unit Cubes

These interlocking, transparent unit cubes work very well for the Warm-Up activity in Activity 2: Money Matters! They are easy to link together and stay together well when displaying the hand span measures.

Delta Education
P.O. Box 3000
Nashua, NH 03061-3000
Phone: (800) 442-5444
FAX: (800) 282-9560
Web: www.delta-ed.com

Individual View Through Components
100 Blue Units   #63-021-2035 $3.60

Centimeter Cubes

Brightly colored, interlocking, plastic cubes each measure 1 cubic centimeter and weigh one 1 gram. These cubes can be used for the Warm-Up activity in Activity 2: Money Matters! They can also be used to build models for the combination problems throughout *Math on the Menu*.

Educators Outlet
P.O. Box 397
Timnath, CO 80547
Phone: (800) 315-2212
FAX: (970) 224-3822

Bucket of 1,000   # 11140 $21.95

Learning Resources
380 N. Fairway Drive
Vernon Hills, IL 60061
Phone: (800) 222-3909
FAX: (800) 222-0249

Set of 500   # LER 0305H $18.95
Set of 1,000   # LER 0305 $34.95

Additional Mathematics Manipulatives
Throughout *Math on the Menu*, there are suggested manipulatives to assist students with problem solving. The materials that are available to your students on a regular basis are recommended.

If you are interested in purchasing unifix cubes, colored wooden or plastic cubes, or other materials, the above sources as well as the source listed below carry standard mathematics manipulatives.

The Math Learning Center
P.O. Box 3226
Salem, OR 97302
Phone: (800) 575-8130
FAX: (503) 370-7961

Resources

Resources for Students

Corn Is Maize: The Gift of the Indians, Aliki, HarperCollins, New York, 1976. This "Let's Read and Find Out" book provides accessible scientific and historical information on corn cultivation and the cultural significance of corn and corn products to indigenous peoples and the world.

Fiestas: Canciones Para Todo El Año, (Holidays: Songs for the Whole Year), Jose Luis Orozco, Arcoiris Records, Inc., P.O. Box 7428, Berkeley, CA 94707 (www.joseluisorozco.com). This is one in a series of many fine recordings by this well-known young people's singer and storyteller whose performances and recordings have helped bring wider cultural understanding to schools and communities nationwide. The Fiestas recording seems particularly appropriate for this unit-it could be played, for example, during the fiesta activity. Dr. Roberto Cruz of the National Advisory Council on Bilingual Education calls Orozco's recordings, "a must for every classroom."

The Kids' Multicultural Cookbook: Food & Fun Around the World, Deanna F. Cook, Williamson Publishing, Charlotte, Vermont, 1995.

Kitchen Science: A Guide to Knowing the Hows and Whys for Fun and Success in the Kitchen, Howard Hillman, Lisa Loring, and Kyle MacDonald, Houghton Mifflin, Boston, 1989.

Passport on a Plate: A Round-the-World Cookbook for Children, Diane Simone Vezza, Simon & Schuster Books for Young Readers, New York, 1997.

The People of Mexico and Their Food, Ann L. Burckhardt, Capstone Press, Mankato, Minnesota, 1996.

Piñatas and Smiling Skeletons: Celebrating Mexican Festivals, Zoe Harris and Suzanne Williams, Pacific View Press, Berkeley, California, 1998.

Resources for Teachers

Discrete Mathematics Across the Curriculum, K–12, 1991 Yearbook, Margaret J. Kenney and Christian R. Hirsch, editors, National Council of Teachers of Mathematics, Reston, Virginia, 1991.

Discrete Mathematics through Applications, Nancy Crisler, Patience Fisher, and Gary Froelich, W.H. Freeman, New York, 1994.

Measuring: From Paces to Feet (part of the Used Numbers: Real Data in the Classroom series), a unit of study for grades 3–4, Rebecca B. Corwin and Susan Jo Russell, Dale Seymour Publications, Palo Alto, California, 1990.

The Multicultural Math Classroom: Bringing in the World, Claudia Zaslavsky, Heinemann, Portsmouth, New Hampshire, 1995.

Principles and Standards for School Mathematics: Discussion Draft, October 1998, National Council of Teachers of Mathematics, Reston, Virginia, 1998.

Professional Standards for Teaching Mathematics, National Council of Teachers of Mathematics, Reston, Virginia, 1991.

Spatial Problem Solving with Cuisenaire Rods, by Patricia S. Davidson and Robert E. Willcutt, Cuisenaire, New Rochelle, New York, 1983.

Statistics: Middles, Means, and In-Betweens (part of the Used Numbers: Real Data in the Classroom series), a unit of study for grades 5–6, Susan N. Friel, Janice R. Mokros, and Susan Jo Russell, Dale Seymour Publications, Palo Alto, California, 1992.

Statistics: Prediction and Sampling (part of the Used Numbers: Real Data in the Classroom series), a unit of study for grades 5–6, Rebecca B. Corwin and Susan N. Friel, Dale Seymour Publications, Palo Alto, California, 1990.

Statistics: The Shape of the Data, Grade 4, Susan Jo Russell, Rebecca B. Corwin, Andee Rubin, and Joan Akers, Dale Seymour Publications, Palo Alto, California, 1995.

Assessment Suggestions

Selected Student Outcomes

1. Students understand what a combination is and know that combinations have a finite number of possibilities.

2. Students are able to determine the number of combinations of two or three items, given five or six items from which to choose.

3. Students are able to use organizational tools such as charts, pictures, and/or diagrams to organize data.

4. Students understand what an average is and improve their ability to calculate averages. Students gain experience with data analysis using averages and modes.

5. Students expand their understanding of area, perimeter, spatial problem solving, and measurement.

6. Students improve in their ability to reason and communicate mathematically.

Built-in Assessment Activities

Journals. Each activity has a journal writing component related to its mathematical content. Entries provide assessments of student levels of content understanding in each activity. This information helps inform the teacher how to proceed with curriculum and instruction. (Outcomes 1–6)

The Proof's in the Organization. In Activity 1 students explain their solutions to the class, including an organizational system. As they present, the teacher can assess their level of understanding of combinations and organizational systems, as well as their ability to communicate their reasoning. (Outcomes 1, 2, 3, 6)

Quote A Price. In Activity 2 students use information about the costs involved in making tostadas to suggest a price to charge for any type of tostada. Teachers can assess how students use averages and data analysis to assist them in this process. (Outcomes 3, 4, 6)

Making Combo Plates. In Activity 3 students begin by independently responding to a proposed solution to a combinatorial problem. Their initial responses provide insights into their level of understanding about combinations. Next, students work in pairs to prove and explain their solutions using organizational tools. At each step of this activity, the teacher gains insight into the students' thinking and understanding. (Outcomes 1, 2, 3, 6)

Design A Floor Plan. In Activity 4 students are given the dimensions of a floor and the items that need to be contained in it. Using a set of parameters, students design and record a floor plan. From their work, teachers can assess student ability to solve a spatial problem within the confines of specific measurements that include area and perimeter. (Outcomes 5, 6)

Additional Assessment Ideas

Ice Cream Parlor. This "Going Further" activity, described in detail following Activity 1, is a good assessment of student ability to transfer their knowledge of combinations to a different setting and could be used during or after the unit. The activity is described in detail on page 17. (Outcomes 1, 2, 3, 6)

Sandwich Shop. The Sandwich Shop "Going Further" following Activity 2 on page 36 serves as an excellent assessment of what students have learned up to that point in the unit. The teacher can gauge student progress, and determine how much and what kind of additional practice may be needed. (Outcomes 1, 2, 3, 4, 6)

Recycling. The Recycling "Going Further" at the end of Activity 2 also serves as an assessment of student ability to transfer their knowledge of averaging to a different setting. The activity is described in detail on page 37. (Outcomes 3, 4, 6)

Design A Playground. This activity (described in "Going Further" on page 73) provides an opportunity for students to use visualization spatial sense, measurement, and problem-solving skills in a real-world context. As they apply those skills and concepts developed in Activity 4, the teacher can assess students' understanding of them through their designs and their letters that communicate the rationale behind the designs. (Outcomes 5, 6)

Combo Cats. This "Going Further" for the entire unit (page 87) is particularly challenging and would make an excellent assessment after completion of the unit. If your students are able to provide accurate responses, illustrations, and reasoning for this problem, it is a strong indication that they understand and can grapple successfully with these kinds of combinatorial problems. (Outcomes 1, 2, 3, 6)

Basketball Stats. Have your students organize, represent, describe, and analyze the following sets of data about the number of points scored by one basketball player and the total number of points per game her team scored. Students determine the range, mode(s), median(s), and average for each part of the problem.

> **Chenoa's Points.** In the past twelve games Chenoa has scored the following number of points per game: 23, 19, 25, 20, 17, 24, 16, 27, 21, 24, 22, 26. What is the range of her points per game? Is there a mode(s)? If so, what is it? What is her median number(s) of points? Estimate her average number of points per game and explain how you determined that number. Calculate the average number of points. How close was your estimation to the actual number?

> **Team Average.** In those same games, Chenoa's team scored the following number of total points: 102, 89, 99, 101, 92, 103, 98, 105, 98, 112, 97, 104. What is the range of the team's points per game? Is there a mode(s)? If so, what is it? What is the median number(s) of points? Estimate the team's average number of points per game and explain how you determined that number. Calculate the average number of points. How close was your estimation? (Outcomes 3, 4, 6)

Alex's Bear. Challenge your students to solve this problem. Alex has a teddy bear that he likes to dress up. His bear has four shirts and three pairs of pants. Alex likes his bear to wear different outfits every day.

> **Pants and Shirts.** How many different shirt and pants outfits can Alex dress his bear in before he has to repeat an outfit? Have students explain their answer, using charts, pictures, diagrams, or any other tool to help illustrate their solution, and explain why they are sure there are no other outfits.

> **Top it Off.** If Alex gets two new hats for his bear, how many different outfits that include a shirt, pants, and a hat can he dress his bear in? Have students explain their answer. (Outcomes 1, 2, 3, 6)

Literature Connections

Anno's Three Little Pigs
by Mitsumasa Anno and Tuyosi Mori
The Bodley Head, London. 1986
Grades: 4–8

Socrates, a wolf, attempts to catch one of three pigs for his wife's dinner. These three pigs collectively own five cottages. With the help of his frog friend, the mathematician Pythagoras, Socrates tries to determine the possible cottages the pigs might be in. Illustrations show the many possible locations of the pigs, clearly demonstrating the difference between permutations and combinations. This type of mathematics, known as combinatorial analysis, forms the basis for computer programming and problem solving and this connection is explained on a more advanced level in the back of the book. Also published with the title *Socrates and the Three Little Pigs*.

Bread, Bread, Bread
by Ann Morris; photographs by Ken Heyman
Lothrop, Lee & Shepard Books, New York. 1989
Grades: K–5

This book celebrates the many different kinds of bread and how it may be enjoyed all over the world. It is filled with photographs of the breads as well as the people who eat them.

Days of the Dead
by Kathryn Lasky; photographs by Christopher G. Knight
Hyperion Books for Children, New York. 1994
Grades: 3–7

The photos and text follow a family in Mexico as they celebrate the holiday. The book depicts the food preparations, decorating the family altars, visiting the village market, and cemetery ceremonies of remembrance.

Everybody Bakes Bread
by Norah Dooley; illustrated by Peter J. Thornton
Carolrhoda Books, Minneapolis. 1996
Grades: 1–6

A rainy-day errand takes Carrie to several neighbors' houses. At each one she finds someone baking a different bread, based on their ethnic heritage. Carrie learns about many different kinds of bread, including chapatis, challah, and papusas. Recipes for the breads are included.

Everybody Cooks Rice
by Norah Dooley; illustrated by Peter J. Thornton
Carolrhoda Books, Minneapolis. 1991
Grades: 1–6

A young girl, Carrie, is sent to find her younger brother, Anthony, for dinner. As she walks around the neighborhood asking friends if they've seen Anthony, Carrie discovers that all of her culturally-diverse neighbors use rice in their recipes. Recipes are given for all the dishes being prepared by Carrie's neighbors.

Family Pictures/Cuadros de familia
by Carmen Lomas Garza
Children's Book Press, San Francisco. 1990
Grades: K–6

In bilingual text and paintings, the author describes her experiences growing up in a Hispanic community in Texas. Each two-page spread bears a highly detailed and lively painting with accompanying text describing the scene. The author has written a second book *In My Family (En Mi Familia)* which continues the description of her experiences. It was published in 1996 by Children's Book Press.

Jalapeño Bagels
by Natasha Wing; illustrated by Robert Casilla
Simon & Schuster, New York. 1996
Grades: K–3

For International Day at school, Pablo wants to bring something that reflects the cultures of both his parents. Jalapeño bagels are the tasty blend of his father, a Jewish baker, and his Mexican mother. Recipes for all the items Pablo helps his parents make are included as well as a glossary of Spanish and Yiddish terms.

The Mix and Match Book of Dinosaurs
by George Sanders
Simon & Schuster, New York. 1992
Grades: K–5

Create outrageous animals with this flip book that has the body parts of prehistoric animals. Mix and match the three parts of each animal and see how many unique ones can be formed.

My Little Island
by Frané Lessac
Harper & Row/Lippincott, New York. 1984
Grades: K–4

A young boy goes with his best friend to visit the little Caribbean island where he was born. The book talks about food in the context of place. What people in a certain region do; what they eat; how they live—all told in few words with vibrant and detailed artwork.

Pigs Will Be Pigs
by Amy Axelrod; illustrated by Sharon McGinley-Nally
Simon & Schuster, New York. 1994
(also available through Scholastic Inc., New York)
Grades: 2–4

After finding their refrigerator empty, the hungry Pig family decides to go out to eat. Upon checking his wallet, Mr. Pig finds only one dollar—certainly not enough for the family of four! An exhaustive hunt through their house produces the additional funds for a meal at the Enchanted Enchilada whose menu features Mexican food—including a combination plate special. The book asks the reader to determine how much money the Pigs found as well as how much money was left after they paid their bill. This book ties in well with Activity 3 where students determine combination plates and the cost for each combination. Two other books, *Pigs In The Pantry* and *Pigs On A Blanket*, are also available from the same author and publisher and connect to measurement and time.

Por-gua-can
by Sara Ball
ars edition, Germany. 1985
Grades: K–5

This mini-flap book along with its companion book, **Croc-gu-phant**, allows the reader to create amusing animals by mixing and matching heads, middle sections, and feet of 11 different animals. If you created every possible one, there would be 1320 phantasmagorical animals in all!

Remarkable Animals
by Tony Meevwissen
Orchard Books, New York. 1998
(originally published in Great Britain, 1997)
Grades: K–4

This flip book contains realistic animals that are in three sections so fanciful creatures can be created. Text is also included. Great for upper elementary students.

Saturday Sancocho
(also available in Spanish as **El Sancocho del Sábado**)
by Leyla Torres
Farrar Straus Giroux, New York. 1995
Grades: K–3

Each Saturday Maria Lili loves to make chicken sancocho with her grandparents. One Saturday, however, they discover they have none of the ingredients, only some eggs. Maria Lili's grandmother gathers the eggs to take to market and invites Maria Lili to come along. Maria Lili can't wait to find out how Mama Ana plans to make chicken sancocho with just eggs. The book includes a recipe for chicken sancocho from the author's family.

Spaghetti and Meatballs for All! A Mathematical Story
by Marilyn Burns; illustrated by Debbie Tilley
Scholastic, New York. 1997
Grades: 3–6

The seating for a family reunion gets complicated as people rearrange the tables and chairs to seat additional guests. A great book for presenting ideas about area and perimeter in a real-world context. Includes a discussion of the mathematics involved, and extensions for learning.

The Tamale Quilt
by Jane Tenorio-Coscarelli
1/4 Inch Designs & Publishing, Murrieta, California. 1998
Grades: K–5

When their grandmother comes to visit for Christmas, Rosa and Manuel enjoy her story about the tamale quilt she made. The story doesn't just entertain the children—it teaches them about their history. Several key words of the story are in Spanish. Included in the book are a recipe for tamales and a pattern and instructions for the quilt.

A Taste of the Mexican Market/El Gusto del Mercado Mexicano
by Nancy María Grande Tabor
Charlesbridge, Watertown, Massachusetts. 1996
Grades: K–4

The reader is taken on a visit to a Mexican market and encounters a wide array of food and other household items. The colorful cut-paper illustrations portray a great diversity of food, while the bilingual text provides a creative way to build new vocabulary for early readers of Spanish or English.

The Toothpaste Millionaire
by Jean Merrill; illustrated by Jan Palmer
Houghton Mifflin, Boston. 1972
Grades: 5–8

Twelve-year-old Rufus doesn't start out to become a millionaire—just to make toothpaste. Incensed by the price of a tube of toothpaste, Rufus tries making his own from bicarbonate of soda with peppermint or vanilla flavoring. Assisted by his friend Kate and his math class (which becomes known as Toothpaste 1), his company grows from a laundry room operation to a corporation with stocks and bank loans. An ideal book to illustrate the need for and use of mathematics in real-world problem solving.

The Tortilla Factory
also available in Spanish as **La Tortilleria**
by Gary Paulsen; illustrated by Ruth Wright Paulsen
Harcourt Brace, New York. 1995
Grades: K–4

This book follows the journey corn takes from the seed in the rich black earth to the growing plant to the grain being ground into the flour that makes the tortilla. The tortilla then makes its way to a home where it is eaten and gives strength to a farm worker who plants the seeds again. The warm paintings and lyrical text pay homage to a cycle of life and helps create a deeper appreciation for the food we eat.

Very Mixed-Up Animals
by Ian Jackson
Millbrook Press, Brookfield, Connecticut. 1998
Grades: K–5

Beautiful real-life illustrations of animals with text included at back to provide information on each animal. Great for upper elementary students. Another book, *Very Mixed-Up Dinosaurs,* is also available from the same author and publisher.

Summary Outlines

Activity 1: Tasty Tostadas

Getting Ready

1. Make two overhead transparencies of the Tostada Combinations Chart.

2. Duplicate the Tostada Combinations Chart data sheet so each pair of students will have two charts.

3. Create one set of paper tostada ingredients for each pair of students.

4. Decide on format for writing component (special journals, already existing journals, or paper sheets).

5. Gather overhead transparencies and pens, student data sheets, and paper tostada ingredients, as well as any optional materials.

Creating Tostadas

1. Survey the class about tostadas, asking students if they have eaten them. Have students describe and list ingredients.

2. Tell students about the Rosada family's restaurant. They plan to offer a choice of **five** different tostada toppings.

3. Using the list of ingredients, circle beans, cheese, salsa, lettuce, and olives. If some are missing, add them to the list. These are the five ingredients the restaurant will offer. Customers can select **three** toppings from the choice of five.

4. The Rosadas have asked for student help in determining how many **different** combinations can be made. **Customers cannot have duplicate toppings.**

5. Have student pairs discuss how many possible combinations, share predictions, and explain thinking.

6. Students will work with partners to solve the problem. Show bag of the paper ingredients and explain these can be used as a tool to solve the problem.

7. They can also use any other classroom manipulative to help them. Remind students the tostada needs to have three *different* toppings.

8. Distribute paper ingredients. Circulate and observe as students work on this problem.

Discussing the Combinations

1. When students are finished, hold a discussion. Ask what strategies they used to solve the problem. Ask how many different combinations they made.

2. Focus attention on the Tostada Combinations Chart overhead. Ask for one combination and record it on the chart.

3. Have partners check to see if they have that combination. If not, they can build a tostada with those items.

4. Ask for a different combination. Record it on chart. Have students check that they also have that combination. Continue, calling on different pairs of students. Have the class check to be sure there are no duplicates.

5. When they think there are no other possible combinations, count them. (There are 10, but **don't tell students this!**) Continue problem solving. If students got the 10 combinations, ask them to prove there are no additional ones. If they do not come up with 10, ask them to explain how they can be certain that there are no more.

6. As students work on their explanations, make copies of the Tostada Combinations Chart available.

7. As students work with partners, listen to strategies they use for their proofs. Ask questions to help students clarify their thinking.

The Proof's in the Organizational System

1. When students finish, have them present their solutions. Find out if any other students have a similar solution.

2. Have students with a different strategy present their solutions. Point out that these are multiple solutions to the same problem. After all solutions have been discussed, ask if there is one that seems best and why.

3. As a wrap up, look at the class chart again. Is it organized in a way that helps them interpret the information?

4. Take this opportunity to show students an organizational strategy that can be applied to this problem. Use the second Tostada Combinations Chart as follows:

   a. Record a first tostada of *beans, cheese, salsa.*

   b. Keeping the beans and cheese constant, record the next two possible combinations—*beans, cheese, lettuce*—and *beans, cheese, olives.*

c. Ask what to record next and why. Record *beans, salsa, lettuce*. Follow with *beans, salsa, olives*.

d. Are there more tostadas with beans? [*beans, lettuce, olives*.] How many possible tostadas were made with beans as one ingredient? [6]

e. Ask what should come next in this recording system. Listen to their ideas. Record *cheese, salsa, lettuce*. Ask what would be next. [*cheese, salsa, olives*] Are there other possible tostadas with cheese? [*cheese, lettuce, olives*]

f. Look at the chart. Are there any other possible tostadas that can be made with the five toppings? Why or why not? [There is one last one—*salsa, lettuce, olives*.]

5. Have students discuss the chart with their partners. Pose questions to stimulate their thinking.

6. Assign a journal writing activity.

Activity 2: Money Matters!

Getting Ready

1. Decide if you will do the Warm-Up activity.

2. Make an overhead transparency of the Tostada Ingredient Costs, determine the costs you will use, and record them on the transparency.

3. Once you have determined prices for ingredients, fill them in on the Tostada Cost Chart. Make an overhead transparency and one copy for each pair of students.

4. Decide if you want to have calculators available.

5. Gather the Tostada Ingredient Costs and Tostada Cost Chart overheads, as well as the Tostada Combinations Chart from Activity 1. Also have the overhead pens and student data sheets at hand.

Optional Warm-Up Activity: Hand-Spans

1. Ask students what they know about *averages*. Discuss how averages are used.

2. Have pairs of students compare their hand sizes by measuring hand-to-hand. Have them make observations.

3. Define hand-span. Ask students to estimate their hand-span in centimeters.

4. Listen to their estimates and record them. Have students determine the lowest and highest estimates and discuss the range.

5. Have students estimate the span of your hand. Show how to measure it in centimeter cubes.

6. Distribute containers of cubes and have students measure their hand spans, then compare actual span to estimated span.

7. Have students compare their hand span with other students near them. Do any students share the same span?

8. Determine the shortest hand span. Have that student bring his "train" of cubes to the front of the room where all students can see it.

9. Determine the longest span and have student bring the cube train to the front. The longest and shortest trains represent the range endpoints.

10. Continue by placing the additional trains between the range from shortest to longest.

11. Have students make observations about the data. You may want to introduce the terms *median* and *mode*.

12. Ask students what they think the average span of a hand is. Have partners discuss and share their thinking.

13. Ask how cubes could be used to determine the average. Demonstrate by taking some cubes off longer trains and adding them to shorter trains. Continue until most trains are the same length.

14. Determine the average span. Ask for a way to determine the average without cubes. You may want to use calculators.

15. Ask students who would be interested in this measurement and why. [Manufacturers of sports equipment, clothing, and medical products.]

Session 1: Tostada Cost Analysis

How Much Is That Tostada?

1. Explain that first the Rosada family sold all tostadas for the same price. Now they want to know how much each of the different tostadas costs to prepare, so they can analyze their profits and possibly adjust the cost. They are asking your students to help.

2. Display Tostada Ingredient Costs overhead and point out the ingredient prices. Ask students for the least and most expensive ingredient. Tell students they will work with a partner and use these prices to determine the cost for all the combinations.

3. Put the Tostada Cost Chart on the overhead. Model how to calculate combination costs by filling in the cost of each ingredient for the first combination. Ask students to mentally calculate the total cost then fill it in on the chart.

4. Put the Tostada Combinations Chart from Activity 1 on the overhead for students to refer to as they determine the cost for each combination. Distribute the Tostada Cost Chart data sheet to each pair of students. Circulate as the students are working.

5. When they finish, record the total cost of each combination on the Tostada Cost Chart overhead.

6. Have students make observations about the costs, ask them about ways to organize it, and display one way.

7. Encourage students to note the range, median, and modes.

An "Average" Tostada Cost

1. Have partners discuss what an average is and how averages are used. How would an average help advise the Rosadas.

2. Have students estimate an average cost for the tostada combinations. Listen to their estimates and how they determined them.

3. Ask students to explain how to calculate the average. Have them work with partners to determine the *average* or *mean* cost. Circulate as students work.

4. Ask for the average cost of tostada combinations. Be sure there is consensus on the average cost!

5. Refer back to the cost of the 10 different combinations. Have students note where the average fits into the organized data, particularly how it relates to the center of the data, and any modes.

6. Tell students this average will be used next when students advise the Rosadas on a single price for any combination.

7. Assign a journal writing activity on averages.

Session 2: Setting the Price

Restaurant Pricing

1. Explain that restaurant owners need to charge more than the cost of the ingredients. Ask why. [To cover expenses and make a profit.]

2. Say that the Rosadas need to at least triple the ingredient costs to meet their expenses and make a profit.

3. Display the Tostada Cost Chart overhead. Have students triple the cost of each combination.

4. Circulate as they work. When they finish, have the class agree on the cost for each combination after it is tripled. Record the tripled costs on the overhead below the Total Cost.

Quote A Price!

1. The Rosada family wants to set a standard price for their tostadas. They sell almost an equal number of each combination every day.

2. Have students work in partners to determine a single price to recommend. They need to have a convincing argument and should include numbers, comparisons, and data analysis in their explanations.

3. As students are working, circulate to observe their strategies and the tools that they use.

4. When students are done, have partners make a case for the price that they think the Rosadas should charge. Ask questions that help students articulate their strategies.

5. Assign a journal writing activity.

Activity 3: Combination Plates

Getting Ready

For Session 1:

1. Decide which opening solution your students will respond to—Joaquin's Solution or Juanita's Solution. Make an overhead of the one you select.

2. Make an overhead transparency of the Combination Plate Menu.

3. Duplicate one copy of the Combination Plate Menu per pair of students.

4. Decide which follow-up problem you will give for homework—either Designer Cakes or Pizza Combos! Duplicate one copy for each student.

5. Provide access to manipulatives to build physical representations of the combinations.

For Session 2:

1. After using it for Session 1, write the price of each item on the Combination Plate Menu overhead.

2. Provide "an allowance" for students. For Joaquin's problem, $3.75. For Juanita's problem, $5.50.

3. Duplicate the Solution Combination Chart (Joaquin's or Juanita's) for the problem students did in Session 1 to assist them in calculating the costs for each combination plate. Also make an overhead transparency of the appropriate chart.

Session 1: Making Combo Plates!
(Do EITHER Joaquin's OR Juanita's Solution)

Joaquin's Solution (Combination Plates with two choices)

1. Tell students the Rosada family wants to expand to also feature combination plates with a choice from six specialties: quesadillas, enchiladas, burritos, tamales, tacos, and chiles rellenos. Put the Combination Plate Menu transparency on the overhead.

2. Customers can choose any **two different** items for their combination plates. The family wants to know how many combinations are possible. Joaquin, one of their four children, came up with 12 different combination plates.

3. Put Joaquin's Solution on the overhead and have a student read it to the class. Then, have students write in their journals about why they agree or disagree with Joaquin's solution.

4. When students finish, have them share their ideas.

5. In partners, have students determine and prove how many combination plates there are. Give them free rein to use any materials. Distribute one copy of the Combination Plate Menu to each pair of students.

6. Remind students to prove their thinking to each other. Circulate as students work.

7. When students finish, have volunteers share their solutions. Have each pair of students present their work. Ask if other partners had the same or similar solutions.

8. If students share a new organizational strategy, be sure that everyone understands it.

9. Assign a journal writing activity.

Juanita's Solution (Combination Plates with three choices)

1. Tell students the Rosada family wants to expand to also feature combination plates with a choice from six specialties: quesadillas, enchiladas, burritos, tamales, tacos, and chiles rellenos. Put the Combination Plate Menu transparency on the overhead.

2. Customers can choose **three different** items on their combination plates. The family wants to know how many combinations are possible. Juanita, one of their four children, came up with 18 different combination plates.

3. Put Juanita's Solution on the overhead and have a student read it to the class. Then, have students write in their journals about why they agree or disagree with Juanita's solution.

4. When students finish, have them share their ideas.

5. In partners, have students determine and prove how many combination plates there are. Give them free rein to use any materials. Distribute one copy of the Combination Plate Menu to each pair of students.

6. Remind students to prove their thinking to each other. Circulate as students work.

7. When students finish, have volunteers share their solutions. Have each pair of students present their work. Ask if other partners had the same or similar solutions.

8. If students share a new organizational strategy, be sure that everyone understands it.

9. Assign a journal writing activity.

Homework

Select the appropriate problem for your students and provide ample time for them to complete the problem at home. Schedule time for students to share their work in class.

Session 2: Out to Lunch

1. Tell the class to pretend they are going out to the Rosada's restaurant. Tell them their allowance for lunch.

2. Put the Combination Plate Menu transparency, which includes the prices, on the overhead. Tell students that the prices include tax.

3. Ask students which combination will be the least expensive. Given the prices, can they select any combination?

   a. For students doing **two** combination plates, distribute Joaquin's Solution Combination Chart or refer students back to their earlier class work on this problem in Session 1.

   b. For students doing **three** combination plates, distribute Juanita's Solution Combination Chart or refer students back to their earlier class work on this problem in Session 1.

4. Have student pairs determine how much each combination plate costs and which ones they can purchase given their budget.

5. Circulate and observe as students work.

6. When students finish, record the cost for each combination on the overhead. Have students select the combination plate of their choice and determine if there would be change from their purchase. If so, how much? How many combinations cannot be purchased? How much more money is needed to purchase them?

7. Have students organize the data from least expensive to most expensive combination plate. Ask for observations. Help them identify the range in price, the most commonly occurring prices (modes), and the center of the data (medians).

8. Have students make a graph of the classes' choices of combinations, and calculate the cost of all the combinations selected to determine the class bill.

9. Assign a journal writing activity.

Activity 4: La Fiesta Restaurante

Getting Ready

For Session 1:

1. Prepare sets of restaurant manipulatives for the floor plan.

2. Duplicate three copies of the Restaurant Floor Plan for each pair of students.

3. Duplicate one copy of the City Building Codes for each pair of students.

4. Make a set of restaurant transparencies.

For Session 2:

1. Decide what manipulatives you will make available to assist students as they solve the paint color combination problem. Pairs of students need a minimum of 10 of each color to solve the problem. Rather than provide the exact amount, we recommend 15 of each color.

2. Place the manipulatives in a plastic bag or container to distribute during the activity.

For Session 3:

1. Students again use the Restaurant Floor Plan and paper manipulatives from Session 1.

2. The third copy of the Restaurant Floor Plan made for Session 1 will be used in this session.

Session 1: Designing Floor Plans

Exploring the Floor Space

1. Tell students the Rosada family just purchased a new restaurant larger than *La Tostada Sabrosa*. They are excited about creating a floor plan. They want to look at a variety and seek student assistance.

2. Display the Restaurant Floor Plan overhead. Tell them the name of the new restaurant and that it means the Party Restaurant.

3. Have students make observations about the floor plan. This is a good time to review perimeter and area. Point out the three shaded squares in

one corner of the restaurant (the doorway) and tell students nothing can be placed on these squares.

4. Distribute one copy of the Restaurant Floor Plan and one set of paper restaurant manipulatives to each pair of students.

5. Put the Kitchen overhead on the floor plan. Ask students to determine the dimensions, perimeter, and area using their paper models on the floor plan.

6. Put the Bathroom overhead on the floor plan. Ask students to find the dimensions, perimeter, and area using their paper models.

7. Tell students the Rosadas purchased 11 tables—four that seat up to six people, four that seat up to four people, and three that seat one or two people.

8. Put the Tables overheads on the floor plan. Have students determine the dimensions, perimeter, and area of each table using their paper models.

Enter the Codes

1. Explain that there are city building codes the Rosadas need to follow. Use overheads of kitchen, bathroom, and tables to show the parameters as you explain them.

2. The kitchen can share one or two sides with the perimeter of the restaurant. It can also stand freely in a location inside the restaurant. Demonstrate the three examples of where it can be situated with the Kitchen overhead.

3. The bathroom needs to share one or both sides with the perimeter of the restaurant. Ask for a few locations where it can be situated. Demonstrate on the overhead. Where wouldn't you situate it and why?

4. Put one transparency of each of the three sizes of tables on the floor plan. Demonstrate how only the shortest side of each table can touch the perimeter of the restaurant along the windows and walls. The tables can also be freestanding with a space around their perimeters.

5. There must be one empty square between any two objects. This allows for the chairs around the tables and provides space to move around the restaurant.

6. Display the City Building Codes overhead and review the codes. Distribute a copy of the City Building Codes to each pair to help them keep the parameters in mind.

Design Time!

1. As students begin designing floor plans, circulate and observe.

2. When partners have a plan, have them raise their hands to show it to you. If the plan meets the codes, give them a second Restaurant Floor Plan to record it. If not, have them keep working!

3. Provide time for students to present their floor plans. Encourage them to explain the strategies they used and their rationale for the final placement of the kitchen, bathroom, and tables.

4. Have students save the paper restaurant manipulatives for Session 3. Post the recorded floor plans and have students look for similarities and differences among them.

5. Assign a journal writing activity.

Session 2: Colorful Combinations

Five Paint Chips

1. The Rosada family is having their restaurant painted. Their budget will allow them to use four colors.

2. The painters brought samples in five colors—red, green, blue, yellow, and orange. The family wants to know what four-color combinations are possible.

3. Have students predict how many combinations there will be, discuss it with a partner, and share predictions.

4. Have students work with partners to determine the number of combinations. Let students know what materials are available to assist them.

5. Circulate as students work. As students finish, focus the class for a group discussion.

6. Ask students how many color combinations the family has to choose from. Have pairs of students present their solutions.

7. Come to consensus about the number of combinations that can be proved using a chart or another strategy.

Adding One More Choice to the Mix!

1. Tell students the Rosadas wanted to see the color combinations if they added one more color choice—purple.

2. With six colors available—red, green, yellow, blue, orange, and purple— how many distinct four-color combinations can they choose from?

3. Have students discuss this with a partner. Listen to their predictions. Be sure they explain their thinking.

4. Have partners work on this problem. Circulate as students work.

5. Focus the class for a group discussion.

6. After everyone has presented solutions, review the various strategies to organize combinations.

7. Assign a journal writing activity.

Session 3: Rave Restaurant Reviews

Big Crowds for Dinner!

1. Tell students that the new restaurant has become very popular. The Rosadas have decided to take reservations—especially since some larger groups have arrived recently, and their table set up has made it difficult to accommodate them.

2. Using their paper models of the tables, bathroom, kitchen, and the restaurant floor plan from Session 1, have students arrange the tables so there is one table for eight, and also other tables close enough to each other so they could accommodate eight at a moment's notice.

3. Have partners work on this problem. Circulate and observe how students approach this challenge.

4. Provide time for students to share strategies and solutions using the restaurant transparencies.

Everybody Loves Saturday Night!

1. Tell students that on a recent Saturday night the Rosadas received reservations.

2. Using their revised floor plans with at least one table for eight from "Big Crowds..." above, have students decide the tables for placing these customers. (Mention that more people will arrive without reservations and possibly even another party of eight or more!)

3. Tell students that beyond creating the floor plan, they should explain how it meets the changing number of diners and why they think it is the best floor plan.

4. As partners work together, circulate and observe.

5. Distribute the third Restaurant Floor Plan for students to record their revised plan.

6. Provide time for students to share their strategies and solutions using the overhead transparency models.

7. Assign a journal writing activity.

Activity 5: Fiesta Time! (Optional)

Tostada Fiesta For Your Class ONLY!

• Students determine the toppings they want on their tostadas.

• Class determines number of toppings allowed on each tostada.

• Based on the number of people who want each topping, students determine the quantity of each topping to buy. Be sure one group also researches the cost of the fried tortillas!

• Students share their research information with team members. As a group, they determine an average serving size for the topping. Based on the number of people who want that topping, they will know the total quantity needed.

• When all groups determine the cost of their individual toppings, find the total cost for all toppings and tortillas. Discuss how to pay for the fiesta.

Tostada Fiesta For Your Class and Their Families

• If you want to include families, follow a similar procedure as above. Students survey their families about what toppings they want. The totals determine how much to buy.

- In addition, students determine where to hold the party and make sure that there is adequate seating.

- Or, you could arrange a more informal tostada party.

Combination Plate Fiestas

- This type of fiesta lends itself to a potluck meal and serves as a unifying way for your students' families to get together.